Crumbs © 2017 by Rose White

All rights reserved. No part of this publication may be reproduced, distributed, or transmitted in any form or by any means, including photocopying, recording, or other electronic or mechanical methods, without the prior written permission of the publisher or author, except in the case of brief quotations embodied in critical reviews and certain other noncommercial uses permitted by copyright law. For permission requests, email the publisher or author at addresses below:

**Contact the author:**
twitter: @rosekellywhite  |  email: rosekellywhite@gmail.com  |  instagram: rosekellywhite

**Contact the publisher:**
Unprecedented Press LLC - 495 Sleepy Hollow Ln, Holland, MI 49423
www.unprecedentedpress.com  |  info@unprecedentedpress.com
twitter: @UnprecdntdPress  |  instagram: unprecedentedpress

ISBN-10: 0-9987602-0-X
ISBN-13: 978-0-9987602-0-9

Printed in the United States of America
Ingram Printing & Distribution, 2017
Edited by Michael White, Jeff Huber and Joshua Best

First Edition

Unprecedented
Press

# CRUMBS
## Rose White

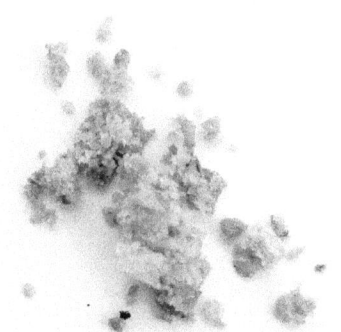

# TABLE OF CONTENTS

| | |
|---|---|
| Introduction | 7 |
| Growing Pains: *Stories about childhood* | 9 |
| The Daily Grind: *Stories about the day to day* | 45 |
| Hit the Road: *Stories about cars* | 87 |
| Schooled: *Stories from the classroom* | 107 |
| Barrel of Monkeys: *Stories about fun times* | 137 |
| My Bad: *Stories about embarassing moments* | 163 |
| Living Things: *Stories about pets and animals* | 187 |
| Going Places: *Stories about travel* | 205 |
| | |
| About The Author | 242 |
| Everyone Global Giving Fund | 243 |
| Other Titles | 244 |

*Crumbs wouldn't have been possible without the contributions of 100 people who shared their stories with me. This book is dedicated to everyone who is in this book and who let me write up their stories. Thanks for letting me badger you until you gave me a story.*

# ACKNOWLEDGEMENTS

Michael White and Jeff Huber were my editors for this book. They took the time to edit 100 stories. That's dedication.

Josh Best visualized Crumbs, paginated it, and turned it into a book. A+ work Josh.

Thanks to Unprecedented Press for taking this book on.

Also, thanks to Lauren Moura who was my 100 Day Project accountability partner.

Shout out to my parents and siblings who allowed to me get stories off all of them during the week of my sister's wedding. Gunnar & Marilyn White, Josh, April, Frederick & Edith Best, Kevin & Carolynn Sylvester, Michael White & Lauren Emmi, and Heidi White & Abel Stewart — you guys are the real heroes.

# INTRODUCTION

In 2015, I challenged myself to write 100 stories in 100 days, but I didn't want to just write about my life or the things that happen to me. I wanted to get these stories from 100 different people in order to turn their everyday stories into something with meaning.

Autobiographies and memoirs typically come from famous people or professional writers. As readers, we accept this because they have a story to tell. These books tell stories that are inherently interesting because of the person or because of complex ideas being artfully communicated.

But perhaps stories don't need to come from a famous person or voice to be special. These are the stories I want to tell. The unusual personal anecdotes that seem insignificant, but someone remembers them. The sharp, colorful memories that maybe only one person can picture.

Everyone's life is filled with stories. Every single day, stories are created: either significant or insignificant. These are the tales told over the phone or dinner. The ones that constitute your life, day in and day out.

So here are 100 stories from 100 people. Some of the stories are momentous, and others are not. But every single story is significant to someone.

This book gives the everyday a platform. It elevates the norm. It highlights the ordinary.

These stories are simply crumbs—small pieces of one person's memory. Maybe they seem insignificant, but a collection of crumbs makes a cookie. And cookies are delicious.

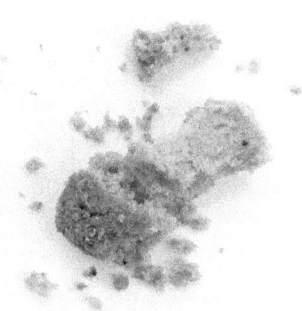

# GROWING PAINS

Stories about childhood

**NATHAN**

**CRUMBS** by Rose White

Summer nights in Northern Michigan are often filled with mosquitos, bonfires, and fireworks. On one of these evenings, Nathan's dad invited some friends over. One boy had never been to Nathan's lakeside house, but he, Nathan, and Nathan's younger brother knew how to pass the time.

They grabbed an armful of fireworks, from sparklers to a type of water-skimming firecrackers. The group lit one of the boat fireworks and pushed it into the water, where it branched off into a number of explosives. They launched into the sky, and then drifted down, sizzling on the water's surface.

The visiting boy snatched another one, swiped a match on the side of the box, and a small flame erupted. He pushed the firework into the water, but it didn't get very far before the explosions started. One of the small flares curved as it soared back onto the shore and swiped the Nathan's brother on his face. The young boy screamed in pain, clutching his face. Nathan rushed him inside and quickly put ice on the burn.

The injury healed over the rest of the summer, into the fall, throughout the winter, and had become a small pink scar underneath his eye by the time all the snow had melted. Nearly a year later, Nathan and his brother had a new firework method: they would rub all the powder off of sparklers, put it in an empty, yellow Play-Doh container, then light it on fire.

Nathan struck a match, dropped it on the pile of explosives, turned in the other direction, and ran. He put his arm around his brother, and they both watched as star-like fire bursts shot out of the old can. The light reflected off Nathan's eyes and shined off the scar on his brother's face.

**CRUMBS** by Rose White

At the fragile age of 8, Mara was taller than most of her classmates. She also typically wore sparkly clothes. Needless to say, she stood out. And this was the evidence Mara proudly displayed, showing that she was different from everyone else.

Because of the glittery bows she wore in her hair, the large sparkly necklaces, the bedazzled shirts, and her frosted bracelets, Mara thought she was a princess. In fact, she thought that she didn't even belong in her regular school and at her regular house with her regular parents.

Mara was convinced that she was so sparkly and glittery that one Christmas Eve when Santa was packing his sled, he accidently took Mara with him mistaking her for one of his wrapped shimmering presents. Then, he dropped her off in Michigan with her parents where she had grown up.

This year, though, Mara was certain that Santa was coming to take her back to her real home, a large castle in the North Pole. Mara was ready to go back and ready to return to her extraordinary home, probably a glittery, tall mansion filled with diamonds and dresses.

But, on the last day of school before Christmas break, Mara and her Fourth grade classmates were ushered inside after a brisk recess. Their teacher sat them down and calmly explained that Santa was not real. At first, Mara wouldn't believe it. Santa was coming back for her this year. But, as her teacher continued, Mara began to realize the truth. She was devastated.

That year, Mara locked herself in her room, and refused to help decorate the tree. To her, Christmas was dead.

# JENSEN

Jensen draped the long cape over his back, throwing it over his shoulders and tying it neatly around his neck. The thin fabric gathered on the ground, brushing against his worn tennis shoes. Jensen then put a mask over his eyes; he stretched the elastic band behind his head and released it with a quiet snap.

Jensen was getting ready for a superhero themed Vacation Bible School. Although his costume was a little mismatched, and his cape was a little too big, when Jensen looked it the mirror, he saw Batman.

Running around a small city display, Jensen saw other kids in similar costumes. He darted in between columns, swishing his cape as he rounded corners. Then, Jensen saw an opportunity: there was a small landing that he could jump off of to grab onto a small pole that was several feet in the air. It was something Batman would definitely do.

He climbed up onto the landing and launched himself into the air. His hands reached out to grab the pole. Caught in suspension, Jensen felt even more like Batman. But, then his hands hit the pole and slid off. He fell to the ground, and broke his wrist.

It was a rude awakening that even Batman could be hurt.

# FREDERICK

Wrrrrhhh.

Frederick made a loud bulldozer noise, and the blocks toppled to the ground. He pushed them all to one side of the room, stacked them again, and wrrrrrh. They fell over again.

Frederick laid his head down on the ground for a second, then remembered he wasn't tired. Back to the bulldozer.

Before long, it was naptime. He did not want to take a nap. So, he and his Aunt Rose read Toy Story 2. The inspector is the bad guy. Then, he got into bed, and they started reading Animal Mechanics.

Wait. Where's monkey! Oh. Right here. Where's deer! Oh, right here.

Aunt Rose tucked him in, told him a story, walked out, and closed the door. But Frederick didn't want to go to sleep. He lay in bed for a minute then yelled, "Aunt Ose!"

...

"Aunt Ose! I hot!"

She came up, turned the fan on, and opened the window. But, he still didn't want to go to bed. A couple of minutes later, his sister Edith started crying. Frederick heard Aunt Rose come upstairs and go into Edith's room.

He waited, and then came out. "Aunt Ose, I scared."

"What are you scared of Frederick?"

"I scared of the minions."

He climbed into the rocking chair, and all three of them read a book. The circles under Frederick's eyes got darker, but he still did not want to go to sleep.

They went back into his room; he climbed into bed, and cried "No! Downstairs!"

**CRUMBS** by Rose White

Frederick listened to his Aunt Rose tell him a story, then watched her walk out, close the door, and heard her pat down the stairs, as he stubbornly continued to fight sleep.

But with the whirr of his fan and the warmth of his blanket, his eyes slowly started to close.

# KEZIA

Kezia sat on the couch watching her older brothers play video games together. She was just a kid, not wanting to be left out. So she grabbed an apple off the counter. Hoping to impress her older brother Keane, she ate the apple as fast as she could. Then, she looked at the core and had a great idea.

If I eat this, Keane will think I'm cool, Kezia thought, so she started to munch on the hard core and swallowed some of the seeds. Keane looked over at her, and he asked, "Kezia, what are you doing?"

"Eating this apple core," she replied.

Keane glanced down at the mangled apple core and said, "You know, if you eat the seeds you'll die."

Kezia stared at him as the fear started the creep into her belly. Her grip on the apple loosened.

Keane continued, "Yeah, we had another brother named Matthew before you were born. He ate some apple seeds and died when a tree grew out of his stomach."

Kezia felt her stomach lurch, and her eyes widened. The fear that an apple tree would grow out of her stomach consumed Kezia. She started crying and didn't stop.

The fear of apple seeds plagued Kezia for weeks. It was quite some time before she ate another apple.

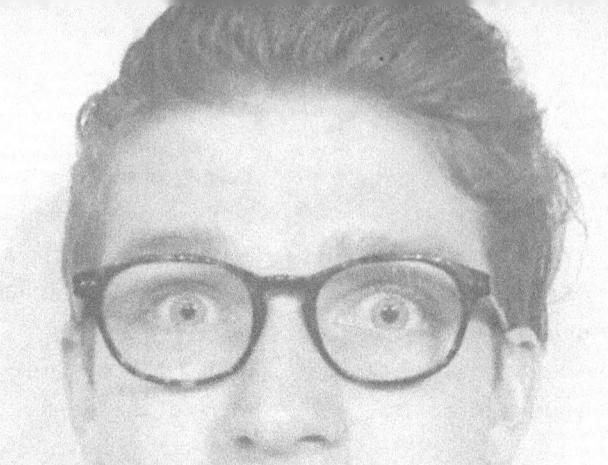

It was a sleepy summer afternoon—the kind that seemed to stretch into eternity. Jamison slid open the back door, and the light rolling sound of the small wheels on the screen indicated possibility. Jamison was wearing an old t-shirt, shorts that stopped just below the knees, and some dark Crocs. With the strap of the rubber shoe behind his heel, he ran out into the grass and headed for the chicken coop.

The roosters were quite territorial: pecking at the hens, jumping on each other's backs, and attacking anything that came near. They were the Woodstock, IL equivalent of raptors in Jurassic Park.

Jamison wandered over to where the birds were and stopped at a seemingly safe distance. He watched the hens cluck, peck the crowd, and shakily walk around. He also watched the roosters, stalking and brooding. The crickets chirped in the background and a small breeze tousled the birds' feathers.

Jamison took a few steps closer, when one of the roosters jerked its head toward him. It began to charge, zipping over the lawn barely lifting its three-toed feet off the ground. It squawked.

The rooster lunged. But Jamison drew back his Croc-ed foot just in time and kicked it. The angry bird was lifted slightly off the ground, then landed a few feet away. It began to run at him again. Jamison kicked it. It landed. It ran. Kicked. Landed. Ran.

After a couple of hard knocks, Jamison saw no sign of defeat in the rooster. He began to get scared. He kicked it one last time, then turned and ran back toward the house. He ran as fast as he could, hoping to escape the rooster.

Finally, he reached the door, whipped it open, and slammed it shut. The accelerated rolling of the screen closing signalled safety.

# KATIE

Making money at the age of 8 can be a difficult venture. But, Katie was able to secure a steady income by walking her neighbor's dog.

She would get $1 per walk: 50 cents for taking it up the road and 50 cents for bringing it back.

One day, she set out with the dog and wrapped the leash around her hand. The two made an unusual pair—a child-sized Katie plus the large horse-like dog. However, they soon entered into their usual rhythm.

After trotting for a couple of minutes, the dog saw a squirrel, or maybe it was a chipmunk, or just a leaf blowing in the wind. Regardless, he took off. In the split second between walking and running, Katie tried to free her hand from the grip of the leash. There wasn't enough time.

As the dog ran, Katie's hand was trapped, and she couldn't keep up. The dog kept chasing something, while dragging poor Katie behind him. Her arm slid across the ground, scraping off skin and picking up dirt. It wasn't until the dog stopped, that she freed her hand, complete with a broken finger.

They had only walked halfway, but Katie started to head back. She put the leash in her good hand and escorted the dog home. Blood and grime coated one arm, while the other knocked on her neighbor's door. He greeted the dog, and let him in. Realizing she had only walked part of the path, the man reached into his pocket and pulled out two dull quarters. He dropped them into Katie's expectant hand, and she ran away.

Katie went to a nearby store and got some candy with her fortune. Then to the hospital for a cast.

JEN

The sun shone through small gaps in the thick canopy of leaves above Jen's head. As she rode her bike down the path, the light from the sun danced on her dark, tanned arms. Jen pedaled fast, the breeze blew her hair back from her face, and she smiled.

She could hear her older brother chasing her on his bike, so she stood up and started to pedal even faster. As she coasted down a looming hill, she turned her head to look over one shoulder. She had outraced her brother.

As Jen turned back around, she saw an elderly woman slowly tottering right in front of her. There was no time to stop. Jen squeezed her left hand hard, trying to brake to no avail. The speed Jen had accumulated on the hill had been too much. Jen clipped the old woman, causing the lady to fall on her face.

Jen jumped off her bike, letting it fall to the ground while yelling, "I'm so sorry! I'm so sorry!" The woman looked up at her, and calmly said, "It's ok." Jen looked up at the elderly woman's companion, probably her daughter whose response was less calm. This woman's eyebrows were cinched together, her arms were crossed, and she scowled, "Look what you've done."

Fear and dread filled Jen's heart. She ran home, abandoning her bike at the scene. She fled into her house, slammed the front door, dashed up the stairs, slammed her bedroom door, and sat on the ground fearing that the cops were going to come and take her away. The fun of riding her bike deflated, and she stayed away from it for a least a week.

# EDITH

CRUMBS by Rose White

The turtle lazily swam through the tank, pushing the water down with its webbed feet, which propelled it forward. It coasted throughout the tank as two young children approached it. Frederick pointed at it, while Edith struggled to stand on the oddly shaped couch that was pushed against the tall tank. The seat curved up and down, giving the young kids the chance to peer into the water.

She put one foot on the couch, grabbed the small ledge lining the tank, and slowly brought herself up to her two feet. Immediately, Edith saw her reflection in the mirror-like murky waters. She smiled at it. The turtle swam above her head, and she laughed at her own face unaware of the creature's proximity.

Suddenly, she realized that her aunt was no longer standing behind her. She turned her head around quickly, searching for the familiar face. Instead, Edith only saw rows of books. Her eyebrows turned downward, and she started to lower herself when Frederick said happily, "Aunt Ose!"

Edith turned back around and searched. Through the waters she saw the face of her aunt. Edith's eyebrows straightened out, and her mouth curved into a smile. Pushing against the glass, she tried to reach her aunt, but the tank was blocking them. Then her aunt rounded the corner, hiding from Edith. Her smile froze until her aunt popped out.

Edith laughed, as she sat down hard. The curvy couch was not prepared for such an abrupt motion, so Edith rolled off. Everything was in motion, especially her aunt hurrying towards her. But soon everything stopped. With a thump, Edith landed on her back. Fortunately, many tumbles off couches, stairs, and beds had prepared her for this.

Meanwhile, the turtle still swam slowly throughout the tank, hardly noticing the quick movements of a fall, a small whimper, and quick recovery.

# ABEL

CRUMBS by Rose White

As a young kid, Abel often went over to his friend's house. One day, he walked into his friend's bedroom and his nose crinkled. It smelled bad. Abel thought, maybe it's just how it smells today, so he just let it be.

The next day, he went back, and it still smelled. Abel's eyes started to water.

"Dude. It smells bad in here."

"It's just my laundry," his friend said as he motioned toward his overflowing laundry basket.

"It smells like a wet poopy diaper!" Abel exclaimed.

His friend shrugged his shoulders.

Abel's face was disgusted. "Dude, I can't be here. I'll see you tomorrow."

Finally on the third day, they didn't even go into the room. Instead, the friends started playing with Nerf guns around the house. In an attempt to hide from his friend, Abel ran into the bedroom and pushed the door closed. He went behind the door in case it opened.

The room smelled worse than it had the day before. Abel held his nose and looked at the ground. Balled up in the corner behind the door was a pair of pure white underwear with a pile of poo in it.

His friend came in and Abel was pointing at the evidence. He yelled, "What is that!"

His friend replied, "I didn't want my mom to find it."

Abel's eyes opened wide, and he called out for the mom to come. She saw the underwear, and Abel's friend's lip started to quiver in embarrassment.

His mom looked at the waste, and she said, "I wouldn't get mad at you for your accident, but you will get in trouble for hiding it!"

Abel went home relieved that his friend's room wouldn't smell anymore.

**MITCH**

Mitch sat in the van with his arms crossed. He didn't want to go to the lake, but his grandmother had gotten him in the van and was driving him there. When they arrived, she opened her door and said, "Come on, Mitch." But, he just wanted to go home.

He didn't budge or unbuckle himself until his grandmother slid open the back door, popped his seatbelt off, and pulled him out of the van. He begrudgingly followed behind her, until she found a spot on the sandy shores to settle down.

Mitch sat down with her and stared out at the lake—he just wanted to go home. He stood up and started to walk around. He kicked pebbles as he wandered around the beach. One small gray rock rolled in front of him.

Looking around, Mitch spotted something bright red. As he got closer, he realized it was a phone. This was his chance to go back home. The emergency phone was perched atop a mound of large boulders, but Mitch didn't let that stop him.

He stretched his leg up and pulled himself onto the first rock. He grabbed the next one and swung his legs on top of it. Quickly, Mitch clambered over the rest of the rocks and reached the phone.

He pulled it off the receiver and dialed 9-1-1. But Mitch knew he couldn't just say that his grandmother forced him to go to the beach.

"911, what is your emergency?"

"My grandmother is trying to kill me."

Mitch hung up the phone. He walked back to where his grandmother was resting and waited. A couple of minutes later the police whipped into the parking lot. They hurried to the lake, saw Mitch sitting calmly with his grandmother, and approached them.

The cops soon realized Mitch was not serious, but that didn't alleviate his grandmother's embarrassment. As soon as the cops left the beach, Mitch's grandmother grabbed their stuff, snatched Mitch's hand, and rushed to the van. They drove home, Mitch smiled, and his grandmother frowned.

# KENDRA

**CRUMBS** by Rose White

Little Kendra sat in the backyard playing with some colorful toys. The thick green grass tickled her legs, but it didn't stop her from pushing some cars around. She felt a little rumble in her stomach, so she looked around the yard.

Near some trees, Kendra saw a clump of flat, brown mushrooms. They looked like cookies. So, she picked one and started munching. Kendra took one big bite, chewing the spongy brown mushroom. The illusion of it being a cookie continued, so Kendra took another bite.

And she took another and another. Bite by bite, Kendra ate the big mushroom cookie. As she neared the end of it, a small rind remained. As Kendra chewed on one of her last bites, her mom came outside and saw the mushroom remnants in Kendra's hand.

"I found a cookie," Kendra said in a small voice. Kendra's mom's eyes widened, and she gasped a little.

She ran forward, ripped it out of Kendra's hand, and threw it on the ground. She picked Kendra up and ran her inside. Hurrying, her mom grabbed a brown bottle and forced a large swallow of ipecac down Kendra's throat. Then she dialed poison control while Kendra started to feel sick.

After a couple of swallows of the thick black syrup, Kendra threw up her first and last mushroom.

# GUSTAVO

Gustavo could feel his friend running up behind him as they raced. Gustavo heard his feet slapping against the concrete, and he could almost feel the warm breath that came from his rapid inhaling and exhaling. Barreling forward, Gustavo tried to increase his speed to increase his distance.

In that moment, the other boy latched his hand onto Gustavo's collar, clamped his fingers together, and ripped his arm back. Gustavo was yanked backward, and he fell to the ground. His head landed hard against the concrete, but Gustavo's pain was exemplified in losing the race.

Leaping to his feet, Gustavo charged toward the other boy, smiling in his victory. Gustavo pulled his arm back and pushed it through the air, punching the other boy right in the nose. His head jerked backward, and he clutched his face. Blood seeped through his fingers and fell down his arms.

A group of older boys walked by the two in their squabble. They saw the other boy crying in pain. His tears mixed with the blood on his face as he yelled, "I'm going to get you!" Gustavo backed away from the boy, feeling smug by defeating the cheater. Then, the other boys pantsed Gustavo.

His pants were at his ankles, the friend was still clutching his face, and the group of older boys chuckled and walked away. Gustavo quickly pulled his pants back up and walked home.

**CRUMBS** by Rose White

When Amber was in elementary school her uncle and grandma lived with her family. Her grandma stayed with them because she had Alzheimer's, but Amber loved her with her whole heart.

It was a warm day, and the sun beat down on Amber and her sister as they played in the backyard. They ran over the bright green grass, playing some kind of game. Amber heard the sound of the backdoor opening, but she just kept playing.

Her uncle walked over to them with a tight smile on his face. He put his hand over his eyes, shielding them from the sun as he looked down on them. Amber looked up and he said, "Amber, your Grandma went out for a walk, and we can't find her."

Amber felt her heart accelerate. Her grandma wouldn't be able to find her way back to the house. So Amber and her sister jumped on their bikes and set out to find her lost grandma.

They pedaled urgently down the street, yelling "Grandma! Grandma! Grandma where are you!" The rode around the neighborhood, still shouting "Grandma!"

After a couple of hours, Amber and her sister returned home nearly crying in their fear. "We couldn't find Grandma," Amber told their Uncle as a couple of tears left streaks in the dirt on her face.

Amber's Uncle just grinned at her and said, "She was here the whole time!" Amber wiped her face with her sleeve, ran to her Grandma, and hugged her tightly around the waist while her Uncle chuckled in the corner, proud of his prank.

# AARON

**CRUMBS** by Rose White

It was the first summer that Aaron's neighborhood had a local pool, and it was the first day he was going to swim in it. He jumped out of his bed, peered out the window, and saw the sun rising with ease. He grabbed his swim trunks and jumped down the stairs.

By mid-morning, Aaron, his dad, his siblings, and his cousins were all headed to the pool. The kids talked about how big they thought the slide was, how deep the pool was, and how tall the diving board was. Aaron thought to himself, it's going to be a good day.

The group walked through the gate to the pool, and Aaron looked around in wonder. It was a massive pool with tons of stuff to explore. Aaron's dad led them to a section where they could start to unload their stuff. Everyone put on sunscreen, but Aaron was too excited.

He threw his stuff on the ground and started to dart around the pool area. Soon, he climbed up a small cement block over the pool area by his family. Aaron's dad wasn't far off, but he had his back turned, helping one of Aaron's siblings put sunscreen on. Aaron yelled to his dad, "I'm gonna jump!"

He launched off the cement, soaring through the air for a short period of time. It happened too fast for Aaron's dad to turn around and notice the young boy. As Aaron came close to his dad, his chin hit his dad's shoulder. It pushed it up, slamming his bottom jaw into his top teeth.

One tooth shattered with the impact, and Aaron grabbed his face. He started bleeding, and he picked up the small tooth fragments. Quickly, Aaron's dad gathered the rest of the kids, put their clothes back on, and they left the pool before the sun had fully risen.

Aaron felt a pit in his stomach form at the thought of ruining everyone's day. After dropping the other kids off at home, Aaron's dad brought him to the hospital where doctors took the rest of the tooth out.

They left the hospital, and the sun was beating down on them. As Aaron's dad drove him home, Aaron had a fresh gap in his smile and a Popsicle for his troubles.

# THE DAILY GRIND

Stories about the day to day

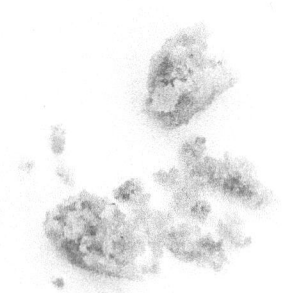

MORGAN

Morgan slipped her feet into her running shoes, tightened the laces, and tied them in a neat bow. She pushed the door open, and it slammed behind her. After stretching for a few minutes in the driveway, she started to run.

She systematically put one foot in front of the other, increasing her stride as she went. Her feet thumped against the pavement—each step a satisfying thud. Morgan slipped into a familiar rhythm, focusing only the sidewalk ahead of her.

As Morgan rounded a corner, she saw a little boy playing in his front yard. He formed a gun with his hand and pretended to shoot things. Bang. The tree. Bang. The mailbox. Bang. The front door.

Morgan ran past him and out of the corner of her eye, she saw his arm following her. She took a few steps, and the boy closed one eye. He cocked the thumb-part of his hand gun, and said, "bang!"

Morgan dropped to the ground and pretended to die. She dramatically made a few dying noises, then she laid still. There were a few seconds of silence until the boy yelled, "Mom. Mom! MOM!" Then he ran inside mortified.

Morgan casually got up, brushed the dirt off her shorts, and finished her run.

# JOSH & APRIL

## APRIL

In the thick of April's first semester at university, Josh asked April if she wanted to go out for dinner. They had been dating for three years, and now they were both in their first years' of school in Toronto. So, when the evening came, April travelled in from the outskirts of the city. She took a bus, then the subway, and made it downtown.

April met up with Josh, and the two walked through the bustling city hand-in-hand. After a brisk stroll, they arrived at the CN Tower, which, at the time, was the tallest building in the world. April tipped her head all the way back, her gaze following the building as it extended into the gray sky.

They went into the building and made their way up to the restaurant situated at the top of the tower. April sat down across from Josh and wondered if he was going to propose at dinner. But, they ate their dinner like any other, only difference was the restaurant slowly rotated around giving guests a full view of the city. After they had circled around a couple of times, April ate the best chocolate mousse of her life.

Josh suggested, "Let's go up to the sky deck, so we can see the city better." April still wondered if Josh was going to propose that night, because as first-year university students, neither of their budgets stretched very far. Then, they walked out and toward the railing. April gazed out at the lights, which illuminated the darkness of the night. Josh then said, "let's go around and meet in the middle."

April started walking, but Josh was not on the other side. So she kept circling the top of the tower, until she found Josh on one knee holding a ring. People were wandering around them, looking out at the Toronto skyline. But April walked past them toward Josh, not knowing how to react. So, she also got down on one knee and said yes.

## JOSH

Living in Toronto as a college student can be rough, and Josh was broke. He often ran out of food between paychecks, and he relied on what remaining snacks he might have like mustard and rice sandwiches. However, he did save enough money to buy April a ring and to take them both out to dinner at the CN Tower, without sparing any expense.

He stood outside the massive structure, waiting for April to meet up with him. He was wearing a sharp, brown jacket, with an engagement ring in the pocket. Josh paced while he waited. Finally, when she arrived, he walked them towards the tower.

Josh knew he was going to propose, so he was shaky and nervous the whole night. He managed to get through dinner, and he ate the best dessert of his life. The restaurant had made several full rotations before he asked April if she wanted to head up to the sky deck, where they would be able to see the whole city.

April chatted, as Josh looked out over Toronto, his stomach reeling with nerves. He didn't know how to segue into a proposal, so he suggested that they walked the tower around then meet in the middle. As soon as April was out of view, he reached into his pocket, pulled out the ring, and got down on one knee.

His knee rested on the cold ground, and he waited for April to round the corner. As soon as she did, he said, "April, will you marry me?" She also got down on one knee. Josh said, "This isn't how this works." She got back up and said yes.

# LAUREN

**CRUMBS** by Rose White

Lauren and her sister Amber stood at the Jet's counter, waiting for their pizza and salad. Finally, the employee in his red shirt and red hat handed a red box to Lauren. She held it carefully as the heat from the fresh pizza emanated through the thin cardboard, warming her hands.

Eager to eat, the sisters strode out of the store—the pizza in front of Lauren, Lauren in front of Amber, and Amber holding the door. Being quite hungry, Lauren walked toward the blue Honda Element, grabbed the handle of the passenger door, opened it, and slowly slid into her seat.

As she eased the door closed without disrupting the pizza, Lauren waited for Amber to also get in the car. But, then she looked out the front window. Lauren saw Amber laughing. Confused, Lauren's eyes passed over the Jet's store and saw the red-shirted employees laughing.

Finally, Lauren looked around the car, and she realized it was not Amber's cube-like vehicle. She quickly got out with her head down and hurried over to the other Honda Element in the parking lot while the delivery man stood by his car.

As she sat down in the proper vehicle, Lauren's face was as red as the pizza box.

Michael spent two months in Ranger school for the Army. It was two months of sleep deprivation, food deprivation, and carrying around a heavy backpack. Toward the end of the school, Michael was exhausted from this prolonged period without proper sleep.

One night, he was a part of a small team that was sent to scope out an objective for an upcoming mission. It was the middle of the night, deep into the woods, and Michael was with a couple of other Rangers who were walking through the woods to complete this task.

Michael felt the weight of his backpack on his shoulders, and the utter darkness of the woods was a comfort. As he walked, he blinked slowly. When he opened eyes, he was still walking, but alone. He looked into the blackness hoping to see one of his team members, but there was nothing.

Now, the darkness enveloped him and became more of an obstacle than a friend. Michael heard a noise off to his left, and he looked over there hoping it was the rest of his group. All of the sudden, a Ranger instructor came into Michael's sight, and he barked "Ranger. Where's the rest of the leader's recon?"

Michael blinked again, still feeling overcome with tiredness. And he replied, "I honestly have no idea."

"Alright, follow me, Ranger."

Both Michael and the instructor walked further into the woods for several minutes. They then heard the rustle of the rest of the team, and Michael joined them again. He rubbed his eyes and focused on the Ranger in front of him for the rest of the mission.

# NERYS

**CRUMBS** by Rose White

Nerys was staying on a friend's couch in Leicester for a couple of days, and it had been a late night. Everyone else in the house had already headed to bed. She heard the last of the creaking floorboards as her friends climbed into their beds, and she finished brushing her teeth. She flicked the bathroom light off and headed to the living room.

Nerys pulled back the blanket on the couch bed and sat down. After she carefully arranged her pillows and sheets, she leaned over and turned the bedside lamp off. There was still a little bit of light coming in from the street, leaving grand shadows on the walls. But they wouldn't bother Nerys.

As she lay there for a couple of minutes with her eyes closed, she suddenly felt the house start shaking. Her eyes jolted open, maybe it was just someone rumbling around upstairs. But, the shaking continued. Nerys looked up at a picture hanging above her head, and it rattled against the wall.

For at least a full minute, Nerys lay on the couch in the dim light watching items around the house shudder slightly. Then, it stopped, and everything was still. Nerys lay on the couch, thinking that it must have been an earthquake.

In the morning, Nerys almost forgot about the strange shaking. But as she drank her morning cup of tea, she remembered. Nerys told her friend about the rumbling and her earthquake conclusion. But, her friend just shook her head.

"It couldn't be an earthquake. It was probably just someone walking around."

Nerys knew it wasn't that, but she looked at her friend's disbelieving eyes. It wasn't worth arguing about even though Nerys knew what had happened to her.

Later that day, Nerys' phone rang. It was her friend. When she answered the phone, her friend excitedly talked about the earthquake that hit their area of England. Nerys smiled, appreciating the confirmation.

# ELIANNA

The streets of New York have a lot of interesting things to observe: colorful pedestrians, loud musicians, elaborate storefronts. But when Elianna walked down the street, those bright and brilliant displays were secondary to one small store window. In this shop was one beautiful accordion that transfixed Elianna.

The large white, gold, and black accordion patiently sat in the shop window as thousands of New Yorkers streamed by day after day. But when Elianna passed the shop her long strides slowed as she neared the accordion.

Like Holly Golightly from Breakfast at Tiffany's, Elianna would peer into the window, and her eyes would run over the small white buttons, the wide golden bellows, and the clean black and white keys. While she gazed at the instrument, she could almost hear happy French bistro music start to play.

Every time Elianna strolled by, she imagined playing that accordion. For months, she looked at it and contemplated purchasing it. Even after leaving New York, she never forgot about that gleaming instrument.

Months later, Elianna still couldn't stop thinking about the accordion. One day, this longing motivated her to track one down. And she did. She found an accordion, got it tuned, and started taking lessons. She slowly learned how to expand and collapse the small accordion, as the waltz music she had imagined poured out of the old instrument.

# KEVIN

**CRUMBS** by Rose White

It's common to find teenagers spending their summers baking in the sun on a hot golf course working as caddies. For Kevin, he spent the three months between school years wearing tan khaki shorts, a white polo, clean tennis shoes, a long red bib with an emblazoned crest, a white towel tossed over his shoulder, and a safari helmet. The outfits were complex, but it made a 15-year-old Kevin look professional.

The thick tan helmet was required for all caddies because of the urban legend that one young caddy was hit in the head with a golf ball and died.

Kevin performed many of the typical caddy jobs, but on invitational days, each caddy was given one job. His job was to sit on the side of the golf course and wait until a ball soared into his area. If it didn't land on the fairway, he would get out of his chair, walk over to it, and put a flag down. Then, he would stand there until the golfer came to retrieve the ball. Finally, he would sit back down and wait. This was his responsibility for 15 hours a day over three-day weekends.

There was another caddy who everyone called Sunshine because of his long blonde hair. Sunshine got one of the worst jobs. He was supposed to sit at one hole and watch every player come by. His only job was to be on the lookout for any player who got a hole-in-one. If a player did, he got a brand new F-150. Needless to say, this was not a common occurrence.

While the sun beat down on the golfers and the caddies, Sunshine sat in his chair listening to music. The heat soon lulled him into a nap. He woke up abruptly when someone got an unprecedented hole-in-one.

But Sunshine wasn't watching, so no one could prove the prize-winning hit. The golfer did not win the truck, the 14-year old was fired on the spot, and the rest of the caddies—Kevin included—carried on with their mundane tasks.

Never had a hole-in-one caused so much misery.

# KEOINA

The room was in chaos, but everyone had their role. Keoina stood next to her best friend who lay in the hospital bed preparing to have her baby. The doctors stood at the end of the bed, the soon-to-be grandparents waited on the other side of the bed, the husband and soon-to-be father stood next to Keoina.

Keoina looked at her friend who she had known since they were kids. She had thin layer of sweat on her face, and she scrunched her eyebrows together in pain. The doctors told her to push, and she did. Keoina rubbed her friend's hand.

While her friend was in the battle of delivery, Keoina smiled thinking of how long they had been friends. After several minutes, the mother gave one last push and yelled. The doctors saw the head and started to pull out the baby.

The baby emerged, and Keoina looked at the little girl in the doctor's hands. Her eyes were closed, her hands were in fists, and her mouth was open in a cry—she was beautiful. The nurses quickly wiped the baby girl off, wrapped her up, and handed her to her mother.

The baby went around the room, being held by her dad, her grandma, her aunt, and then she came to Keoina. The small, warm bundle was placed in Keoina's arms. Nothing but her face poked out of the clean, white blanket. Keoina looked at her perfectly smooth face and smiled without breathing, but thinking, this is incredible.

SUSAN

Susan pulled her phone out of her purse and saw the bright alert, "Missed Call." After realizing she didn't recognize the phone number, Susan politely texted the person with a simple "I'm not sure who this is, but did you need something from me?"

The number responded saying "It's Drew, and I called to talk to you about the magazine photo shoot. You can check out my website." Susan still didn't know who the person was, but she decided to take a look at the site. The mystery caller turned out to be an established, critically acclaimed photographer in Britain.

Susan typed out on her phone "I think you have the wrong number, but your work looks great!" For no good reason the conversation continued beyond awkward embarrassment. The man explained that he was calling the editor of the magazine, but he typed in one wrong digit.

They continued texting about the photographer's work, the shoot coming up, and more. Eventually, they started talking on the phone. The caller had a lovely, deep, rich voice, and he seemed like a great guy. He told Susan about the photo shoot, and he asked her if she would like to come and help out. Naturally, she agreed, eager to meet the mysterious photographer with a great voice.

As Susan made her way to the location, the man called her. He explained that he and his team were going to be late to the shoot and asked Susan to explain the delay to the clients. She arrived, being the only representative of the photography team and attempted to validate the lateness. She said something about the team scouting out another location. As time passed, the clients and Susan were both anxiously awaiting the arrival of the photographer.

**CRUMBS** by Rose White

Eventually, the team walked through the door. Was he the tall one? Was he the one with the nice hair? Then, she heard his voice. She looked around searching for the source, then her gaze dropped down to a stout balding man. The quality of his voice did not seem to match the person containing it. Even as he spoke, Susan still saw the man she had pictured him to be. But the shoot went on, and Susan was able to help out at this high-level photo shoot by moving lights, holding camera equipment, and helping the models. It was the best day of work she had ever had.

Sometimes, a single digit goes a long way.

# DAVE

When Dave was working as a driving instructor in Wales, he came to appreciate the roadside rest stops. They didn't offer much, but they allowed any casual passerby to stop in, do their business, and be on their way without having to go into the city.

Where Dave lived and often drove, there were four of these rest stops. It was a simple set up: a tall wall and a small building that offered privacy and a place for relief. However, after some time, these convenient stops started to close. Naturally, this chagrined Dave, but he learned to adapt.

In a casual conversation with a friend who happened to be a reporter, Dave talked to her about how he often used the rest stops, and how they were being shut down. He disclosed this information solely on the basis of a friendly chat, but it came back.

That week, the local newspaper came out, and printed in the dark, heavy text was a bold headline, "Local Businessman Upset Over Closing Urinals." Surprised, Dave read the piece to discover that his complaint about the rest stops had now been published.

After that, Dave learned not to tell things like that to writers.

# CHRISTINA

**CRUMBS** by Rose White

Christina stood at the door of the Children's Museum while the sounds of kids running, yelling in excitement, and playing with toys echoed around her. She smiled when a family started to approach the doors.

The little boy ran up to the front of the museum and started tugging on the short Kids Only door. He ran inside, saw Christina, and wrapped his arms around her legs. He gripped her in a tight hug and looked up with wide, excited eyes.

He hurried over to a large car, climbed in, and beckoned for Christina to come over. She walked over to where he sat and talked to him as he drove the car. Then, they both ran around on the first floor for some time before heading upstairs.

While the little boy played, Christina leaned against the wall. Occasionally, she would look around the museum or start talking to a co-worker. Every time she did, the boy ran up to her silently begging for her attention.

After some time on the second floor, the two started to play Eye Spy. They stood on the balcony looking down at the colorful bustle below them. Christina saw her friend Duncan below them, so she said, "I spy a guy." The little boy peered down, until he saw Duncan, "Right there!" he yelled.

Christina happily replied, "You're right! That's my friend Duncan; can you say 'Hi Duncan!'"

The little boy whipped his arm back and forth in an enthusiastic wave and yelled, "Hi pumpkin!"

The game continued, but every round the little boy shouted, "I spy…a bus!" while Christina pointed out the cars parked below them. They played this until the boy had to leave. Christina walked down with the boy and his family, waving as he walked out the small kids door in the waiting "bus."

## CRUMBS by Rose White

On a sticky late August evening, Logan played a show with his band at a bar called Mulligan's. It had been one of those days where the heat seemed to slow time down. Even though the sun had set, Logan could still feel the heat in the crowded room.

Logan and his band started playing, and the night went on. While on the stage, he peered into the packed room and saw people dancing, following traditional concert etiquette.

The show went well, but the combination of a Michigan August, a crowd of people, and playing under hot lights made Logan sweaty. The salty water seemed to emanate from every pore. The show wrapped up, and Logan wiped the moisture off his face in relief.

Without taking a break to cool down, Logan started to tear down the equipment—thus inciting a new wave of sweat. He packed away instruments, moved amps, and walked back and forth from Mulligan's to the car.

In the middle of this process, a bohemian-looking girl wearing a flowing patterned skirt and a loose top walked up to Logan. She pointed at his arm and asked, "Is that a new tattoo?"

They both looked at the colorful explosion on his forearm, and he replied, "I got it a couple of months ago."

At that moment, the girl grabbed Logan's sweaty arm, brought it up to her face, inhaled deeply, and said, "I really like it," then walked away from Logan and his quiet disbelief.

A stranger just smelled his perspiring, non-freshly tattooed arm.

ANONYMOUS

*The person in this story wanted to remain unidentified, so she'll be called Anonymous for the purposes of the narrative.

Anonymous met a friend for coffee. She had already had a couple of cups that day, but one more wouldn't hurt. She drank her iced beverage quickly. The two chatted casually, but Anonymous started to shift in her seat. Moving around, she scanned the room for a bathroom.

The two friends said a quick goodbye, giving each other a hug. Anonymous debated running to a bathroom, but her hatred of public bathrooms motivated her to go home. It's a short drive, she thought hopefully.

As she steered her car home, every bump in the road, every sudden stop, and every pothole was torture. She sped up.

Finally, Anonymous reached her house. She whipped open the door, running to the bathroom. But, the door was shut. Her roommate had locked the door. It can't really be much longer, she hoped.

She walked carefully to her room, sat on her bed, and crossed her legs in an attempt to stall the waterfall trying to get out. After a couple of minutes she heard the shower come on. Her heart sank. She couldn't wait that long.

After looking around for a few minutes, she ran out of her room, grabbed a large bowl, and hurried back to her room. She closed the door and locked it. Then, she squatted over the bowl in relief.

Anonymous picked the bowl up, walking slowly toward the kitchen. She could still hear the happy hum of the shower as her feet padded carefully across the carpet. She dumped her waste into the sink and turned the faucet all the way to red until steam started to rise.

## CRUMBS by Rose White

She put the bowl under the water letting it fill with scalding water and dumping it out several times. Then she grabbed a sponge, filled it with soap, and rubbed the bowl out again, and again, and again.

Anonymous picked up a towel, dried the bowl off, and put it back in the cupboard.

Later that night, Anonymous returned home to find her roommates watching a movie. She started to ask, "what movie are you—" when she saw the bowl. It was filled with popcorn. She quickly said goodnight to her roommates and fled to her room in horror. They were eating popcorn out of her pee bowl. She would never tell her secret.

# CAROLYNN & KEVIN

## CRUMBS by Rose White

After coming back from a long camping trip in Montana with a group of rowdy highschoolers, Carolynn received a text from her supervisor, Kevin.

It read: "How adventurous and spontaneous are you?"

Carolynn replied, "Does it involve camping?" At this point, all she wanted to do was sleep in her own bed.

But Kevin's response read, "Yes."

Even though it did involve sleeping on the ground, Carolynn still decided to go.

She didn't find out until later that day that they would be going to Denver for the weekend to see Old Crow and the Avett Brothers. It would be an eight-hour car ride and the first time that Kevin and Carolynn spent time together outside of work.

The two took off in Kevin's car excited for the concert and excited for the road trip from Billings to Denver. A couple of hours in, the two were happily chatting when Kevin's car started to overheat. He pulled over to the side of the road, let it cool down, and kept driving.

A little while later, it happened again, and he pulled over before driving again. This process repeated itself over and over and over. Finally after 14 hours, Kevin and Carolynn made it to Denver. They met up with some friends before the concert and talked about the drive.

"So did you guys listen to Old Crow and the Avett Brothers on the way down?" The other couple asked them.

Carolynn and Kevin looked at each other and shook their heads as they looked back at the couple. "No, we just talked."

Then, the group headed to the concert. Afterward, Carolynn and Kevin went back to the campground where they were staying for the night. They were sharing a small 8ft x 8ft

**CRUMBS** by Rose White

area and had set up their tents already. There was barely a walkable aisle between the two tents. Before heading to their separate tents, Carolynn and Kevin talked.

After a couple of minutes, they kissed. Kevin was nervous, so he quickly patted Carolynn on both her arms and said goodnight. Then they both went into their tents silently, heard each other zip their tent doors closed, and settle down for the night.

Without a word they climbed into their separate sleeping bags, rolled onto their sides, smiled, and focused on sleep and not on the flimsy tent walls that couldn't muffle a rustle.

Two years later, they were married.

# ROSE

It was Day 87 of a 100-day project around 8:30pm, and Rose scanned the crowded room. She walked over to a girl named Kristen and started casually chatting. The 100 Days Project came up, and Rose said, "I'm pretty excited to be done. It's been fun, but I'm ready." Kristen nodded, and they kept talking about it. Then, the conversation naturally shifted toward travelling.

Rose tilted her head and narrowed her eyes slightly, "So, do you have any stories? About travelling?"

Kristen paused for a moment, looked to the side, and launched into her story about a flight to Amsterdam. She excitedly shared the narrative as Rose took small notes in her phone. She typed single words at a time to spark her memory later.

When Kristen finished sharing the story, Rose asked, "Can I take your picture?" She looked around the room searching for a suitable backdrop. She pinched her eyebrows together and said, "Maybe, we'll go outside."

The two walked out a door that read "Emergency Exit," but luckily there was no alarm. Rose pushed on the door, and it opened relatively quietly. SHe looked at Kristen as they walked and casually started to say, "I don't think—"

Then Rose fell down a step that she didn't know was there. Her ankles folded, then her knees gave way, and she landed on her knees and rolled onto the ground. She started to stand up and looked around. About 10 feet away a car sat at a stop sign; the windows were down and two guys stared out. They weren't laughing, pointing—nothing.

Rose then looked at Kristen and started laughing. "How did that happen?" Kristen kept laughing, and finally, the car pulled away as the guys yelled out something indiscriminate. Rose then looked inside and

**CRUMBS** by Rose White

three girls were just staring. When they saw Rose laughing, they opened the door with smiles. "Are you okay?"

Rose rolled up her pants and showed everyone her knees. Although the pants were intact, her knees had been scraped raw. She laughed even harder.

It took 100 days to collect and write 100 stories. And it all ended with one skinned knee.

# HIT THE ROAD

Stories about cars

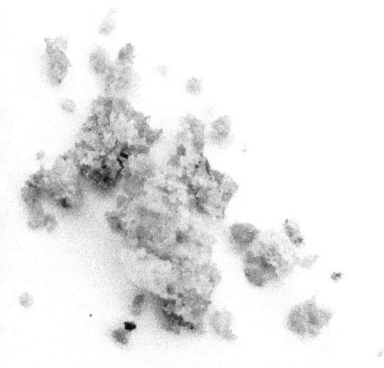

# OLIVIA

Olivia hurried out of the house, yanked the nearly frozen VW Cabrio convertible door open, rammed the key in the ignition, and started her car. She spun the heat dial all the way up, turned on her defroster, and started the butt warmer.

Several minutes later, Olivia was bundled up and ready to go. She walked out the door into the morning darkness. Exhaling, Olivia watched a white cloud of vapor leave her body. It felt like she had lost at least an ounce of body heat—forever gone to the frigid air.

Olivia walked over to her car and pulled on the handle, but it would not budge. She pulled and pulled on the handle, but it remained closed. Meanwhile, her car continued to get warmer on the inside, emitting hot, billowing clouds from the exhaust.

She did not know how to get in. Then, she had a thought. For this car, if the driver turned the key in the lock to the left twice, the windows rolled down. She ran back into the house, grabbed her spare key, and put it in the lock. Holding her breath she turned it once. Then, she turned it again. There was the soft noise of windows going down, and Olivia released her breath in a cloud of relief.

She now looked at the small window and had to figure out how to get in. Maybe she could put one foot in and climb in? Nope. Her car was too small. Olivia sat backwards in the window and just slid in, butt first. After all this time and effort, her bum was met with a nice warm greeting.

## CRUMBS by Rose White

The white gauge on Levi's gas meter dipped below the E, but he kept driving until his car started to sputter out. Pulling over into a parking lot of an abandoned building, Levi realized he couldn't get the car anywhere. So he left it there.

A couple of days later, he came back and saw the bright pink police sticker on the window. He put some gas in it but still couldn't get the car to start. So, he left it again. The next time he went to get it, the car was gone.

Levi just assumed that the cops impounded it, so he called the police. He asked where his car went, gave them his license plate number, and was told they didn't have his car. He called the towing company and was told they didn't have his car.

Levi called the police again, this time to report his car stolen. The cops didn't really look into the case of the stolen abandoned car, so Levi started taking things into his own hands. He contacted a friend who knew the streets of Grand Rapids, MI.

The two stopped by all the sketchy scrap yards around the city. They pulled up to one small junk yard, and Levi spotted his car—bright pink sticker and all. Levi called the police one more time. They came and covered it in a thin film of dust, searching for fingerprints.

Because of Levi's investigation, the car was rescued. It was towed out of the scrap yard, escaping an impending fate of being stripped and sold for parts.

**JORDAN**

Riding in a friend's car, Jordan was excited to finally about to get his car back from the shop. His car had been in and out, but every time Jordan picked it up he hoped it would be the last time. Jordan and his friend Mitch pulled into the mechanic's parking lot, and they saw Jordan's shiny black car ready to be driven.

Jordan unlocked the door and slid into the leather seat. He put the key into the ignition and the engine roared. Jordan thought, Sweet! It's running! Then, he started driving away. Looking into his rearview mirror, he saw that Mitch wasn't moving.

Jordan backed up, and Mitch said, "My car isn't starting." So Jordan hopped out of his car, grabbed his jumper cables, and started to jump Mitch's car. The other car started, but Jordan's stopped working. Finally, they managed to get both cars started and headed down the road to a gas station.

They both filled up their cars with gas and got back in the drivers' seats. Both Jordan and Mitch tried to start their cars, but they didn't work. This time, they decided to call a friend. When she got there, she jumped Jordan's car. He left it running while Mitch's car was jumped.

When the other car finally started, Jordan's had just died. They jumped Jordan's, but then Mitch's stopped. Back and forth they went, but they could not keep both cars running at the same time.

Fed up, they went to get new batteries, changed them, and both cars started up easily.

Full of hope and optimism, Jordan drove his car all the way home. As soon as he pulled into the driveway, the car stalled out. Jordan sighed and rested his head on his steering wheel. At least Mitch's car was still running.

# CLARENCE

The bright orange car had gone from being a blur on the highway to stuck in a busy Chicago traffic jam. Clarence's usually speedy demeanor had been replaced by the sluggish start and go of the busy highway.

The windows were down and a slight breeze wafted into the car. Iggy Azalea poured out of the speakers, as honking and the sound of engines attempted to drown her out. The driver and the passenger chatted, while Clarence fell into the rhythm between first gear, neutral, and braking.

Time had stopped moving. But, just when Clarence was ready to exhaust this endless highway, another bright orange car pulled up next to him. It was more of a sports car, but the two shared a sense of solidarity. They were two vibrant orange spots in a sea of bland metallic colors.

The other car pulled ahead, but was still in sight. Then Clarence's lane moved forward, and the other car fell behind. The two drivers waved at each other. For the rest of the traffic jam, the two orange splotches passed each other several times, until Clarence pulled off the highway.

Clarence cherishes being the one and only orange blast, but for a few minutes it was nice to have a friend. No orange is an island.

# JACKIE

While coasting down the road, Jackie and her friends blasted the Pitch Perfect soundtrack. The windows were down and the girls' voices were lost in the roar of the music. Jackie pumped her first in the air, holding the wheel with one hand.

As the car neared the destination driveway, Jackie lowered her foot on the brake. The music kept playing, the passengers kept singing, and Jackie kept dancing. When she saw the entrance to the drive, she started to turn but her focus was still on car-partying.

Jackie gripped the wheel and started to spin in it toward the left. But she turned too soon. The car turned right into a ditch that ran deep alongside the paved drive. The car started to fall on its side; the passengers started to scream.

The vehicle fell, stuck partly on its side. Jackie immediately stopped the song that was coming out of her mouth, her smile was replaced with tears. She climbed out of the car and called for help. It eventually got pulled out of the ditch, and Jackie gave away her CD.

The next time she got her oil changed, the mechanic asked her, "Do you let people borrow your car?" Jackie nodded her head yes, wondering how he knew. He replied, "I think someone took it off-roading."

# CRUMBS by Rose White

It was late. Lydia had already missed her curfew a couple of times, so she grabbed her phone and quickly typed out "Hey Dad. Is it ok if I'm a little late tonight?" She hit send. After waiting a couple of minutes with no response, Lydia thought, it's probably ok.

By the time Lydia was actually heading home, it was nearly 2am. She drove down a narrow two-lane country road with her windows down and the wind whipping her hair. The darkness surrounded her small car, except for the bright beams that illuminated a small section of visibility in front of her.

Lydia looked in her rear view mirror and saw the bright lights of a fire truck coming up behind her. She tried to get out of its way and pulled onto the side of the road. There was almost no space, so Lydia went off the pavement. The fire truck roared past her in a blur of noise and light.

Then, she stepped on the gas and turned her steering wheel to get back on the road. Her car went nowhere. She was stuck in a ditch. Lydia pulled her phone out again and texted her dad, "Now I see why you worry when I'm out late, because I'm literally stuck in a ditch." She then called a friend for help.

They both tried pushing the car out to no avail. After several minutes of just the two of them trying, the fire truck came back down the road. It slowed down by Lydia's car and the driver yelled out the window, "Do you need help?"

"Sure," Lydia responded.

Then six firemen jumped out of the truck in full fire suits. They walked over to Lydia's small car, and began to push. After a couple of minutes they succeeded in releasing the car from the ditch.

Lydia and her car were rescued by the same fireman who led to her getting stuck in the first place.

# LUMP OF CLAY

CRUMBS by Rose White

The lump of clay was hoisted off the ground and lugged to the car. The plastic bag around it rustled in the slight summer breeze, but it kept the clay fresh. The hands gripping the bag held on tight, leaving slight impressions in the soft clay.

The lump was lifted up and placed on top of a small car as the driver unlocked the door. The person opened her door, threw her purse in the back, and slid in. The engine roared to life, and the car started to pull away.

The clay rested on the hood of the car as the bag started to be whipped around the clay. The car continued to drive, merging onto the highway. It picked up speed and the lump of clay struggled to stay on the car.

The clay started to slide down the car, making its way toward the windshield. At that moment, the car started to slow down and clay began to level out again. When the car came to a complete stop, the clay slid a little more, nearing the edge of the roof.

The driver hopped out of the car, grabbed the soft clay, put it in the car, and tucked it in a seat with a seatbelt just in time.

**KEVIN**

Kevin blinked, letting his eyelids droop a little—but not too long. He shook his face, willing himself to stay awake as he completed the last stretch of driving on his whirlwind of a trip. He had taken three high school track runners to from Michigan to North Carolina for the Nationals tournament. He drove 14 hours there, hustled the teenagers around all weekend, and was driving the 14 hours back.

Finally, he felt his stomach fill with relief as he pulled off the highway. Kevin was comforted by the familiarity. One by one, he dropped each of the athletes off at their houses and went to return the van to the head coach's house.

Kevin pulled into the driveway, pressed the button to open the garage door, and pulled in. Parked next to the van in the garage was Kevin's car. He looked at it longingly.

Climbing into his car, Kevin could already feel himself relaxing after the weekend. He couldn't wait to get home. So he backed out of the garage, too tired to even check his blind spots. As his car rolled backward, Kevin heard a crack as his mirror hit the side of the garage. Exhausted, he let it fall off.

Kevin continued to drive home without a mirror. He only lived about a mile away, and the speed limits were slow. Every intersection felt like an eternity, as Kevin dreamt of falling into his bed. Then Kevin heard his tire go out and his car started to grind on the road. He pulled over and put his head on the steering wheel.

Reluctantly, Kevin climbed out of his car and changed his tire. As he lugged the broken one into his trunk, he leaned against the car taking a quick rest. He then sat back in his car and continued the short drive home. Finally, he pulled into his own driveway. Clicking the button on his seatbelt released him from the weekend.

As he climbed out, he looked on top of his car and saw his wallet and his backpack sitting there. He grabbed them, shocked they hadn't fallen off. He laughed to himself. 1,600 problem free miles, ruined by the final mile home. But it was nothing a long nap couldn't fix.

# GUNNAR

CRUMBS by Rose White

In 1983, Gunnar was 25. He spent that summer working in Colorado on a medium-sized horse ranch. He had enjoyed the season there, but the breeze was starting to get cooler, and the earth was starting to get a little browner. Gunnar knew it was time to head back to Michigan.

So, he bought a cool '63 Pontiac Grand Prix for $200 from a friend. Gunnar packed up his new-old car and hit the road. It would be a long drive, but the windows rolled down and the radio worked.

He was one day into the drive, cruising through Iowa when Gunnar spotted a hitchhiker on the road. His hand was outstretched just waiting for someone to stop. So Gunnar pulled the car over to the side of the road, asked the young man where he was going, and offered him a ride.

They drove down the highway chitchatting for a couple of hours when the car started to act up. Gunnar and his passenger realized that the car had run out of oil, so they coasted it down the nearest exit ramp. Parking it on the side of the road, they walked to a nearby K-Mart, bought the oil, and continued on their drive despite the setback.

The rest of the journey back, Gunnar and his new road buddy had to stop several times to get that car more oil. 24 quarts later they arrived in Michigan.

But Gunnar had made it back, and he sold the car a few months later. Despite its oil guzzling tendencies, Gunnar wishes he never got rid of that classic road-trip car. It probably would have rusted over the past 30 years, but Gunnar's memories of driving the old car would remain untarnished.

# SCHOOLED

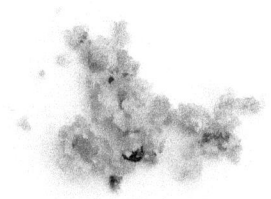

Stories from the classroom

# MELISSA

## CRUMBS by Rose White

The bell rang, and students scurried through the hallways to their classes. After a few minutes of chaos, the bell rang again. The long halls were now empty and quiet except for the muffled sound of teachers talking inside their classrooms.

Melissa padded down the hall, making her way to class. She knew she was late, but with a smile Melissa remembered that her class was supposed to have a sub today. Stopping abruptly in the middle of the hall, Melissa reached into her bag, and her hand dug around. Her fingers moved aside pencils, books, and folders, until they found a small crinkled piece of paper.

Triumphantly, Melissa pulled out an old hall pass. She figured the sub wouldn't look at the date, and the tardiness would not be recognized. Just to be sure, though, Melissa took the cap off a black pen and artfully changed the date. With a smile, she trotted off to class.

Melissa grabbed the handle of the door, and eased it open. She was pleased with her own cleverness. As she walked in, her heart dropped. In her mind she heard three low notes indicating disaster: dun dun duuuuuuuun. Her teacher was there, and Melissa had the hall pass in her hand.

She hurried to her desk and slid in. Her teacher, however, noticed the small slip of white paper in Melissa's hand and asked her, "Melissa, do you have a hall pass?"

Melissa looked at her desk.

"Melissa let me see your hall pass."

"I'll take a late." Melissa assured her teacher.

"No, bring it over."

Melissa slowly got out of her chair, placed the paper on the desk, and watched as her teacher—seemingly in slow motion—reached down to pick it up. Melissa felt the guilt overcome her. Before the teacher looked at it and as the whole class waited in anticipation, Melissa yelled, "It's fake! I tampered with it! It's a fake pass! I'll take myself to the principal's office."

Once again, Melissa found herself walking through the empty hallways. This time, disappointed in her cleverness. She headed straight to the principal's office, entered, and said, "Hi Mr. Gallagher. I'm really sorry I tampered with my hall pass. Do with me as you like." She expected the worst: suspension, detention, expulsion.

But, Mr. Gallagher only smiled slightly and said to Melissa, "You're fine. Go back to class."

NATE

Sixth grade was a good year for Nate. He was funny, cool, and he always had something good to say. Nate spent that year climbing the heights of popularity, but it was also a pivotal year in his education.

One day in his Science class, Nate's teacher was taking them through a lesson on heredity and genetics. She talked about how physical traits, like moustaches, are inherited. While she talked, Nate tried not to focus on the slight moustache that was perfectly situated on his teacher's face.

She was Italian and had dark hair on her head and dark hair on her face. She continued talking about facial hair and its genetic implications. After a couple of minutes, the woman started walking around the room to ensure students understood the topic.

As she approached Nate, he started thinking about genetics, facial hair, and his teacher's dark peach fuzz. He wanted to say to her, as a genetic generalization, you have facial hair. But, when she came up to him, Nate just looked at the dark hair on her lip. He couldn't look away, so he just blurted out "You have facial hair."

She replied, "Yeah, I know." Then, she walked out of the classroom.

Nate immediately felt his face burning as his friend leaned over and said, "Dude!" Nate didn't know if he should apologize, so he didn't say anything.

The next day, she came to school and the moustache was gone. After that, Nate sat in the back of classroom, rarely raised his hand in class, and despised poster projects.

# ALEXIS

In first grade, Alexis was still figuring out the world. She often sat in her classroom and looked out the door to see the Special Education class and the Deaf class, which was across the hall. She didn't really know why they were in a different class, but she could easily see them in their classrooms from where she sat.

Sometimes, Alexis's class would walk by the deaf class in the hallway. She would see the kids with their earpieces and the large boxes that hung around their necks and thought that these lucky kids got to go to school with walkie-talkies. She didn't really understand why they had those things.

One day on the playground, Alexis stood at the top of a tall slide looking down. She could see one of the boys with the special earpiece-walkie-talkie standing on the ground. He was always mad. His eyebrows were scrunched together, and his mouth was turned down.

Alexis slid down the slide, letting the wind blow her hair off her face. She landed with a soft crunch on the small white pebbles. Then, she walked by the grumpy boy and started playing near him. He looked at Alexis and thought she wanted to take what he was playing with. So, he marched over to her and pushed her to the ground.

Alexis fell over onto the ground, and the white dust from the playground pebbles got in her dark hair. She opened her eyes and could just see the angry boy yelling at her, but she couldn't understand a word of what he was saying. Now, she scrunched her eyebrows together in confusion, why was this boy yelling at her?

After he finished shouting, Alexis stood up, brushed herself off, and ran away.

# SHARDAE

When Shardae was eight, she could be a little sassy at times.

She had an odd relationship with a guy in her third grade class named John. It was one of those elementary school relationships that was adverse yet friendly. John and Shardae had a running joke where they would call each other "Pierre" as an insult.

Pierre was just a word that sounded mean to them.

One day, Shardae thought it would sound better in writing, so on a piece of construction paper she wrote "John: Pierre."

Then, Shardae wrote everyone's name in the class and what she thought about them. For some it was ":prince" or ":princess," but for people she didn't like, in her 8-year-old mindset, she write ":witch." Then next to John, she wrote "John: Pierre" again.

Shardae leaned over to John and showed him her handiwork. Like a Pierre, he snatched the paper and showed it to the teacher. Shardae was appalled. She ran away, hid in the bathroom, and came back 10 minutes later.

As a form of third-grade punishment, Shardae had to write an apology and read it in front of the class. Her hands trembled as they held the piece of off-white paper covered with the wide lines ready for cursive practice. Shardae publicly apologized.

Years later, John and Shardae had a class together. One day, he brought up Pierre. Shardae had nearly forgotten. John said, "We used to call each other Pierre, but then you wrote that hit list."

Unknowingly, young Shardae had written a hit list on eight-year-olds. Looking back, she realized that her classmates must have been so scared of her.

DEB

## CRUMBS by Rose White

Masses of people donned their square caps—3,000 of them wearing the same outfit: the dark blue robes with the matching hat. The crowd shared the achievement, but for each one it meant something different. Perhaps there was a Biomedical Sciences major, eager to have one degree under her belt, then maybe there was the English student whose future was uncertain. And there was the Psychology major from Brazil, named Deb. Walking into the auditorium, she tipped her head back and laughed. It was the kind of laugh that is recognizable, even within the rumbling crowd.

The ceremony seemed to drag on, but Snapchat was a faithful companion to Deb. She snapped herself walking in, she snapped the auditorium, she snapped the ceremony. This event would be well documented, even if those photos would eventually disappear. But it didn't matter. After having studied in the United States for five years, Deb was ready to share this with the world. Deep into the expansive auditorium, she was sharing it with the pillars in her life: her parents and her best friends. This was her victory—her prize.

As the ceremony continued, doctoral robes were put on, graduate certificates were given, and then the College of Liberal Arts and Sciences began to stand. Row by row, soon-to-be graduates stood up, straightened their hats, flattened their robes, and walked over to the stage in the dim lighting. If one was going to trip, now would be the time. Deb followed suit and walked behind the robe in front of her.

The closer she got to the stage, the lighter the room became. At the foot of the stairs, she stepped down with her heeled foot on the first stair. She climbed up that step, having conquered the difficulties of being in college with English being her second language. She stepped onto the second step, defeating the rejection she faced after applying for scholarships and jobs but being denied. She stepped on the third one, overcoming the spontaneous but lasting illness that afflicted her sophomore year. Bringing both feet onto the platform, the lights bounced off her dark hair, and she walked over to receive her degree.

This was her dream.

# ASHLEY

Excitedly, Ashley straightened the large white lab coat over her small, kindergarten-sized body. It was dress-what-you-want-to-be-when-you-grow-up day, and Ashley was decked out as a scientist in the white coat with a couple of beakers sticking out of the pockets.

When she got to school all the other kids were dressed up in their career outfits. The day proceeded as normal: the weather, the alphabet, playtime, and coloring. Coloring was Ashley's favorite part of the day.

She pulled her Rose Art markers out of her backpack. She took the cap off a red marker and drew a thick line on a piece of rough construction paper. They weren't the brand name Crayola, but they were good enough.

After coloring for a few minutes, Ashley was careful not to get any marker on her pristine white coat. She drew a few more line sketches, when a kindergarten-sized construction worker named Nate Sunday walked by. He looked at the white Rose Art markers in Ashley's hands, and cruelly said, "Nice markers nerd!"

Ashley looked at the markers in her hand and put them down. She packed them up in her backpack and quietly waited for coloring time to end. Trying not to cry, Ashley looked at the ground, nursing her hurt kindergarten heart.

Ashley moved away from school before going into first grade. Years later, she went back to that district to go to high school. One day, she was walking through the hallway when she saw Nate Sunday. Immediately, she felt a surge of sadness as she remembered the pain he had caused her younger self. Ashley kept the insult to herself, while thinking "You're that mean kid." And she kept walking.

# CAMILLE

CRUMBS by Rose White

Clad in a blue robe and a sharp cap, Camille sat in the rows and rows of soon-to-be graduates. Filled with thousands of people, the arena was hot and stuffy, but it was time for each individual to get their one second of recognition after four years of work.

Camille sat in the cushioned chair, tapping her foot against the air. Up and down, up and down, her heeled foot went, anxiously waiting for her row to stand. Soon, three rows in front of her rose, walked toward the stage, and trotted across the platform. Then, two rows got up, walked, trotted, and sat back down. Then, the row in front of her was filled with vacant seats as her time quickly came.

After having discussed it with some friends, Camille was going to take a selfie with the president of the university, T. Haas. Just like that Eminem song, this was her moment, to own it, to never let it go, because she was getting only one shot, and she did not want to miss her chance.

Camille had her phone ready in one hand and gave the card with her name to the announcer. "Camille C. Nofsinger" rang out in auditorium. Friends and family in the audience cheered, but Camille didn't hear it. Instead she was focused on shaking hands, then she focused on T. Haas.

She drew near and quickly asked him, "Can I take a selfie?" He responded, "Yes. But quickly." She whipped up the small camera icon on her phone, and snapped the photo. In her hurry, she did not realize that T. Haas had not bent down, nor had she slowed down enough to capture a clear image. Instead she was left with a slightly blurry selfie with the chin of the president.

But a photo taken of her taking the selfie was perfectly captured.

# JOLENE

Young kids clambered out of their seats, hurrying to get changed before heading to gym class. The room went from silent to chaotic with the noises of moving chairs, moving kids, and low whispers that grew quickly. The small students rushed over to the closet to get their gym clothes, talking and giggling.

As everyone left the room, Jolene stayed back. She was wearing one of her favorite outfits that day: black snap up pants, athletic shorts, and her Mickey shirt. She stood up and waited for her classmates to return so they could walk to the gym. As she waited, she tapped her shoes on the worn brown carpet, and her eyes traced the long alphabet banner that snaked around the walls.

After a couple of minutes, some of her classmates began to come back into the room, wearing their shorts, t-shirts, and tennis shoes. Jolene knew she didn't have to change, so she gripped the front of her pants with her hands, and whipped them forward. True to their name, her pants made small snapping sounds as the buttons separated.

The pants crumpled to the ground just as Jolene realized she was not wearing any shorts underneath. Quickly, she bent her knees, tugging her shirt down as far as it could go. Helplessly, she held her shirt there and stared at her unsnapped pants, lying on the ground a few feet away.

Jolene's teacher came up to her and said quietly, "I think you forgot something." Then, the kind teacher buttoned the pants back up and Jolene pulled them back on. She followed the rest of her classmates to the gym, still not needing to change out of her current athletic wear.

# RYAN

It was cloudy but still warm enough for Ryan to be kicking around a soccer ball with a classmate during recess. The black and white hexagons swirled around as the ball went back and forth between the two young boys.

They played for a while, until Ryan's friend proclaimed, "I need to pee. Want to pee with me?" Ryan shook his head and replied, "Nope." The other boy walked a short distance away, peed in the grass, and ran back to the playground.

Ryan waited until he had left, then followed suit, and continued to kick around the soccer ball. But, another student had seen Ryan relieve himself in the schoolyard, and he was now running to tell their principal.

Mr. Power was a tall man, some say he was close to 7 feet. As soon as the young student told the principal what he had seen Ryan do, Mr. Power walked over to where Ryan was still playing. Even though the sun wasn't bright, Ryan felt a shadow fall across him. He looked up to see Mr. Power looking down on him, "Ryan, let's take a walk."

The two started to stroll around the playground. Mr. Power took long, slow strides, while Ryan took quick, short strides as he hurried to keep up. Ryan's sense of dread weighed on him, and he started to bawl. Mr. Power could tell Ryan knew that he did something wrong, so he simply said, "Ryan. Don't pee again."

# ARI

As a bright high school student, Ari skipped out on his seventh-hour class to intern with a local PR firm. He spent his afternoons there, but soon got to know the leader of an NGO in the office next door. This man started to ask Ari to do a few things for him:

NGO: Would you like to start doing some data input for me?
Ari: Sure.

NGO: I'm not great at English, so could you start writing some emails for me?
Ari: Sure.

NGO: I have a conference call with the President, could you do it for me?
Ari: …Sure.

The seventeen-year old nervously sat in the small office, looking at the basic, black office phone. There was nothing special about it: curly cord and different lines, but at 3:00pm, it rang.

Ari: Hello, Mr. President. My name is Ari.
President Obama: Hello. It's nice to meet you.

Clearly, Ari was not the person President Obama intended to call, so Ari explained why a high school student was on the phone with the leader of the free world.

Obama: I bet your Dad won't believe this.
Ari: Probably not.

The call continued, and situated from Air Force One, the President asked Ari his opinion about legislation on immigration issues. He answered as best as he could. The conversation ended with a polite: "Ari, you sound like a very nice man."

Ari placed the office phone back into its cradle, looked at his boss, and asked, "What do you think?"

NGO: Good job.

Later that day Ari went home and told his dad about the conversation.

Dad: You talked to the President of what? Student Council?
Ari: Dad, The President of the United States.
Dad: Ari, you're too old to tell lies.

# GRACEY

There was a to-do list for everything.

Gracey took her list out and checked the outside of the plane. Then she picked up another list and checked the inside of the plane. She sat down in the pilot's seat, clicked her seatbelt, and checked everything in front of her. Gracey's instructor sat to her right, and her classmate sat in the back.

This was Gracey's first piloted flight with her aviation high school. She fidgeted with the steering wheel, tapped her foot on the ground, and darted her eyes around the cockpit. She picked up the radio, and with a nod from her instructor, Gracey called to get clearance for takeoff.

When she got the go-ahead, Gracey taxied the plane by pushing down on the large pedals below her feet. Gently, she pressed her left foot down and the plane began to move, then she pressed her right foot down in order to steer it. Left. Right. Left. Right. And she inched towards the runway. When she got to the edge of it, Gracey ran through another checklist.

At last, she began her takeoff. The plane picked up speed as it raced down the runway, then Gracey steered it off the ground and into the sky. She held her breath as the wheels lifted from the earth, and she didn't let it go until she had leveled out.

She released her clenched hands from the steering wheel just slightly, and she felt air blow onto her sweating palms. Her back relaxed into the seat as she looked out the window. She couldn't see her school from here, and it felt like she had flown away from the dozens of checklist items.

For the remainder of her flight, Gracey coasted the plane through bright sky with far fewer restrictions than the road.

# RYAN

## CRUMBS by Rose White

Ryan leaned back in his chair, while his high school cooking teacher stood at the front of the classroom. She started class by talking about desserts, and Ryan responded by crossing his arms and tipping his chair back on two legs.

The teacher went on to mention her cheesecake, saying something like, "I make the best cheesecake." Ryan scoffed—that seemed a little outrageous. To stroke his ego, he decided to pipe up.

"I bet I can make a better cake than you," he challenged his teacher. She reluctantly took him up on the offer. Ryan had never made a cheesecake before.

That afternoon, Ryan went home, turned the computer on, and opened Google. He typed in "cheesecake recipes," and the page loaded more than 6 million results. He barely scrolled down the page and clicked on AllRecipes.com.

His eyes flicked over the page until he saw Chantal's New York Cheesecake—looked good enough. He printed it off and got to work. He set off into the kitchen, gathered the ingredients, and made a cheesecake.

The next morning, Ryan wrapped it carefully and set off to school. He took it to class and his teacher was standing with her cheesecake. She unwrapped it and set it on the counter.

Once everyone was in the class, Ryan and his teacher cut up their cakes into small bites, handed them out, and waited as the other students tried each one. While they ate, Ryan's teacher told them about her cheesecake and how it was made with natural ingredients, whole-wheat flour, and low fat sweetener.

The class took a vote for the cakes. A few students timidly raised their hands for the teacher's cake, and the rest of the class happily raised their hands for Ryan's cake. Ryan smiled, gathered his leftovers, and tromped back to his seat.

Although it was Ryan's first cheesecake, it was not his last. He now proudly says that he makes the best cheesecake, until someone challenges him.

# GRAYSON

Rose: "Grayson, tell me a story"
Grayson: "One time," She paused thoughtfully. "No that's not a good one."

Grayson: "Um. One time…I was in Guatemala. No."

Me: "Ok, maybe just start with 'one time'"

Grayson: "Ok. One time…One time in Fourth grade my teacher made me tell the whole class about when I went to the White House and met the president. It was awful."

Grayson, as a young girl, sat in her teacher's chair peering out at her class. Row after row of desks were filled with students. The chair had been raised to its tallest height, and Grayson tried telling the story while wearing her crisp, grey crewneck sweatshirt emblazoned with 'Washington DC.'

She tried to talk about it without letting her voice shake. "Everything was old, and I saw the green room. I also got presidential M&Ms." Grayson told about her experience with the oval office. She had boldly put one of her small feet, covered in a black pleather boot into the office of the President when no one was looking. Her boots matched the Limited Too pleather jacket she was wearing.

The situation seemed never-ending, as Grayson talked she nervously looked at her class. Some of her peers were looking at her, but their eyes were glazed over. Others were slouched, resting their chin on their hands. Grayson's gaze then shifted to her teacher, who sat on the edge of his seat, completely unaware of the students' boredom.

Grayson didn't get the point of talking about her vacation.

"Nobody cared." Grayson shrugged her shoulders as she finished telling the story of how much she hates telling stories.

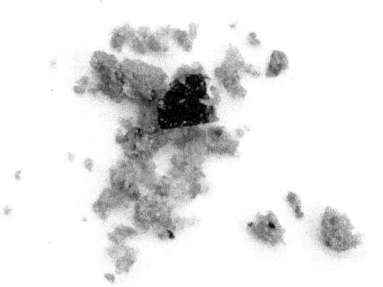

# BARREL OF MONKEYS

Stories about fun times

November 22: the day JFK was assassinated, the day A.A. Milne died, the day C.S. Lewis died, and Anna's birthday. Anna always hated her birthday.

Growing up, Anna was idealistic with high expectations for her birthday. However, within short 9 years, her idealism faded. That year it was forever buried under a thick layer of cynicism.

She woke up on the morning of her 9th birthday and climbed into the shower. She turned the knob and waited for the steam to start rising. But it never did. She started to shower, and the lukewarm water succeeded in only making her colder. Quickly, she got out, and an empty house greeted her. The sound of silence killed any potential birthday greetings.

When Anna arrived home from school that day, her mom kindly asked where she would like to go for dinner. Anna begrudgingly responded with, "Panera." As the two pulled into the parking lot, ready to celebrate the birthday, Anna saw all of her friends from school eating dinner in the bright restaurant. Feeling betrayed, tears spilled from Anna's eyes. Why was everyone hanging out without her? Anna's mom tried to explain that she had planned a surprise party, and all of Anna's friends were there for her, but it was to no avail. Anna had already cried, her eyes had puffed, and she was certain that her birthday was ruined.

After that, Anna's family avoided telling her Happy Birthday, she refused to celebrate, and every year something would happen which would only reinforce her theory that birthdays are terrible: the sweater she wanted to wear would go missing, she would step on an ice cube in a clean sock, or her mom would make the wrong flavor of cake. The years passed and November 22 became a day where Anna's sister would only text to say, "Happy JFK Assassination," as a weak means of remembrance.

However, after Anna's 21st birthday, her mom told her that she was her most wanted child. November 22, the day Anna was born, was a warm, rainy day, and it was the best day of her mom's life. The cynicism began to chip away, as Anna and her mom became friends instead of just mother and daughter. Anna began to think about her birthday as less of an uncomfortable event and more of a celebration of the day her mom gave her something— gave her life. Then, on Anna's 22nd birthday, her golden birthday, she recognized it for the first time in a long time. Now, she was happy for her friend, and she celebrated it as her birthday and her mom's favorite day.

# JEFF

**CRUMBS** by Rose White

The middle of July is often filled with still, hot days. It's hard to be productive, and it's also hard to find something to do. On one of these boiling days, all Jeff and a friend wanted to do was sit in a cold dark theatre drinking iced teas.

Iron Man was playing nearby, so they drove with the windows down and stopped at a nearby gas station for Arizona Raspberry Iced Teas. A couple of minutes later, they pulled into the parking lot of the theatre, realizing they had no way of sneaking their drinks in.

They didn't have any bags, they weren't wearing sweatshirts, and their jeans' pockets were way too small. Like anyone smuggling outside food or drink into the cinema, they wanted to be discrete and at least pretend like the employees didn't know what they were doing.

Squinting in the sun, Jeff looked at the Iced Tea sweating in the heat. Jeff's friend offered to tuck them into the top part of his pants by the belt.

They walked in and purchased their tickets, but the more they walked the farther the teas went down the pant leg. The jeans were tight enough to reveal two can shapes being tightly held against the back of someone's thigh. Jeff saw these two visible bulges from 23 oz cans, so he walked closely behind his friend, mirroring his walking style.

They made it down the long hallway, entered the dim theatre, found a seat, and released the captive Arizona's. Jeff sat down, leaned back in his red chair, cracked open the can, and took a sip. It wasn't quite cold anymore, but it was totally worth it.

# THI

## CRUMBS by Rose White

A thick layer of snow coated the earth, including the white parking lot. Thi and her friends looked out the window as flakes continued to tumble onto the white blanket. While they gazed at the grey skies, someone said, "We should go skitching."

Thi buttoned up her coat, pulled her mittens on, and tromped outside. The car was ready, and the back part of the trunk had been lowered for people to grab ahold of. Thi watched as some people gripped the trunk closure, squatted down, and held on as the small Honda Element drove around the parking lot. In the wake of the car and its passengers, small dark trails were left in the clean snow where feet gouged in drag marks.

Finally, it was Thi's turn. She grabbed on next to Sophie, squatted, and the car drove away. She slid on the snow, skiing without the skis. Suddenly, Sophie slipped off the back of the car and rolled in the snow. Thi started laughing.

She laughed so hard that she peed a little. But once she let a little out, she couldn't hold it in. It was like trying to hold back a waterfall. Quickly reasoning, Thi decided she would roll in the snow to try to cover up her wet pants. So she slowly released her grip on the car, rolled in the snow, and ran inside claiming to go to the bathroom.

No one noticed anything as she got up and walked in. She flicked on the light in the bathroom, lifted up her coat, and realized that her snow plan had not worked. Instead, she was left with a darkened, wet spot on her pants that obviously indicated that she had peed. There was nothing to do now except own up to it.

She ran back outside, lifted her arms in the air, and yelled, "I peed!"

# DENISE

**CRUMBS** by Rose White

Birthdays are supposed to be celebrated and celebrated with people. That was all Denise wanted for this birthday: dinner with her family. She sat in the crowded Bill Knapp's restaurant with her parents, her husband, and her two-year old daughter, Shawnna. As they ate, Denise looked around the table and smiled. Now, all she needed was cake.

As everyone finished their dinners, Shawnna started to get fussy. Denise's husband picked her up and went outside to try to calm her down. A couple of minutes later, Denise's parents went to the restroom.

While they left, Denise sat and smiled as the waiter took her plate away. Denise took a sip of water and leaned back in her chair. At that moment, the restaurant's staff came out singing their birthday song. The whole restaurant turned to look at Denise sitting at the large table by herself.

She slid down a little bit in her chair and uncomfortably waited for the song to finish. Finally, they put a large piece of cake down in front of Denise, wished her a happy birthday, and walked away.

Denise picked up her fork and skimmed the frosting with the tongs, leaving light lines in the white sugar. Then, she looked at the empty chairs and put the fork back down. She flattened the napkin on her lap and looked up to see her husband come back in. Then on the other side of the room, Denise's parents were coming back.

As everyone sat back down, Denise picked up her fork and took a big bite of cake.

# GABE

Nearing the end of spring break, Gabe headed to a small league hockey game with a couple of friends. It had been a long, lonely week because many of Gabe's friends had gone somewhere warm for spring break. Suffering from cabin fever, Gabe was now in a 'why not' mood. He was up for anything.

Gabe and his friends trotted to their seats, which seemed to have put them as far away from the ice as possible. They sat there for the first period while plotting how to get closer. As soon as one of the security officials walked away, Gabe and his friends ran down to the bottom of the arena right by the glass.

A cameraman was situated right by their new seats, and every time he pointed his camera in their direction Gabe would do something. He didn't always get on the big screen, but Gabe kept yelling his name, "Cameraman! Cameraman! Cameraman!"

While waiting for the cameraman to turn around, Gabe had an idea. He unzipped his jacket and unbuttoned his shirt, but held them closed. Finally, when the camera lens came his way, he opened his jacket and started dancing—this time, he was on the big screen. The audience collectively said, "Ooooh!"

After a couple of seconds, the camera panned away, and Gabe zipped his jacket back up relishing the warmth on his cold skin. The weekend passed, and Gabe had mostly forgotten about the event. Then he went to church that Sunday, and a middle-aged mother came up to him.

"Were you at the Griffin's game this weekend?"

"Yeah," he said, still not recalling his five seconds of fame.

Then as Gabe started to remember, she simply said, "We saw your tease."

# KYLE

CRUMBS by Rose White

Voices bounced around the room, young kids ran between tables, people grabbed steamy pieces of pizza letting the cheese slid down, and the late afternoon sun streamed through the windows, immersing some in a bright light and putting others in the shadows. But, everyone was happy.

The chatter continued as the sun continued to drop, until the clear ding of a knife hitting a glass cut through the noise. Kyle and Katie stood at the front of the room, smiling at their friends and family. "First of all, we just want to thank you all for coming out. This is probably only one fifth of who has been there for us." Kyle started to thank the people in the room and talk about the past six months. Katie also joined in, expressing her gratitude.

"Now, I'm just going to address a few frequently asked questions, because we don't want to answer them for each person. First, why do I have hair right now? The nurses don't even know, but one of my friends saw me without hair and prayed, saying, 'God. No.'" Kyle joked, and finished his list of questions: yes he was feeling better, all his medical bills were paid, the last scan would be in a few weeks, and this is the end of this season in his and Katie's life.

When Kyle finished talking, everyone turned back toward each other and the conversations continued. The sun was now parallel with the windows, casting an ending, golden glow on the dark wood in the room. Kyle and Katie stopped at various tables to chat, take a bite of pizza, and block the sun from their eyes.

This was Kyle's first day without chemo.

While studying at a Bible school in Wales, Jed stopped by a Toby Carvery for a Sunday roast with his friend Aaron. The buffet-style restaurant was packed with people, meats, sauces, and gravies. When the two walked in, they scanned the busy room looking for a table.

Aaron pointed at a table already filled with people and said to Jed "That's Robbie Fowler. He was one of the best football players in the country. His nickname is god."

Jed made a quick decision and nervously walked past the table filled with a fat turkey, a large ham, a thick slice of pork, as he headed over to the jams and sauces table. He pretended to check out the selection, while scoping out Robbie Fowler. Jed just wanted a laugh, so he walked up to where Robbie was sitting with his family.

"Mr. Fowler?"

Robbie looked up from his roast, still chewing, and grunted, "Yeah."

"Can I tell you a joke?"

He put another bit of meat into his mouth and nodded his head.

"What do you get with a fish with no eyes?"

Robbie looked at Jed, chewed his food, and easily answered "Fssh."

Jed quickly replied, "Yeah. That's right." And he walked away.

He quickly recanted the experience to Aaron as they filled their plates with meat, vegetables, and yorkshire pudding.

Jed successfully told a joke to god.

# BETHANY

**CRUMBS** by Rose White

Bethany stepped out of her car and quickly walked toward the wedding ceremony. She was wearing a bright green, knee length dress with a teardrop peephole. It highlighted her porcelain skin and made her clear blue eyes pop. As Bethany walked toward the building, she waved at a friend, Jess. The closer she got to her, the slower her wave became. Jess was wearing the exact same dress as Bethany.

Bethany just wanted to go home and change, but the ceremony was about to begin. She sat in her chair, and the procession started. Bridesmaids and groomsmen slowly walked down the aisle, and as person and person walked by, all Bethany could think about was the dress. Then, everyone stood up, and the bride began to walk. People pulled out their tissues, tears dripped, and noses were sniffled, but Bethany could only think about the dress.

At the reception, Bethany plopped down at her table where the most stylish guy from the wedding was also sat. She respected his outfit, while still reviling hers. Pulling out her phone, Bethany quickly caught up on her Twitter feed. A friend had retweeted someone who had posted, "there are two women here with the same dress. How tragic." Compelled by a driving curiosity, she tapped the name of the original tweeter. His twitter loaded, and she recognized the face—it was the stylish man across the table.

With nothing left to lose, Bethany shrugged her shoulders and thought: at least people are talking about me.

# CAITLIN

# CRUMBS by Rose White

Caitlin hurried from house to house wearing a laundry basket with a hole cut in it around her waist. Although she was a 17-year old senior in high school, her and her friends still went trick-or-treating. But this would be the last year.

After hitting up many of the houses in the packed development, Caitlin and her friends parted ways. She hurried home with her laundry basket and pillowcase full of candy. She ran up to her room and saw her other costume lying on her bed. It was a tiger outfit.

She was going out with her boyfriend to a college party. This was not something she usually did—she did not drink, stay out too late, or break any rules, which was precisely her rationale for going out this one time.

Caitlin slipped into her new costume, leaving the now useless laundry basket on the ground. She then picked up a barely used makeup bag, applied eyeliner, mascara, and lipstick.

Once she was done, she ran down the stairs and bumped into her mom. "Where are you going?" Her mom asked.

"I'm spending the night at Chloe's," Caitlin lied. In reality, she probably could have just told her mom the truth, but for some reason she felt a surge of rebellion. She ran out the door and into her boyfriend's car. The two jetted off to the party.

Only a short time after they arrived, Caitlin's phone rang. She looked at the small window on the front, and it was her mom. Her short rebellious streak had faded, and she felt an urge to answer. She flipped open the phone and her mom just said, "You aren't at Chloe's."

Caitlin started crying immediately, apologizing over and over again. Her mom said, "Caitlin. Stop crying. You're probably embarrassing yourself in front of all your friends…Caitlin. Stop crying. We'll talk about it tomorrow morning."

This was the first and last time Caitlin ever got grounded.

# KAITLYN

"You guys want to go out on the paddle boat?" Jared asked Kaitlyn and Camille. Kaitlyn looked out the window, and it seemed completely dark compared to the well-lit room. But, they agreed to go out anyway.

Once outside, Kaitlyn noticed that it wasn't as dark as she thought. The cloudless sky made room for a smattering of stars, which illuminated the night. The moon reflected off the clear water of the lake, making it twice as bright.

They pushed the boat into the water, letting the sound of ripples against the shore fill the stillness of the night. Kaitlyn and Camille paddled while Jared was perched on the end of the boat. "Do you think we will see any fresh water glow-in-the dark jellyfish?" He asked.

Kaitlyn peered into the inky black waters, looking for anything. Then, she heard a rustling noise. Looking into the trees, she tried to determine the maker of the noise. Then, it got louder and a bat flew past the boat.

Scared of the bat, Jared stood up to go to the front of the boat, but he stepped too hard on one side, nearly falling in. He crawled back to the front, scared of standing up again. Kaitlyn kept paddling them around in circles, but Jared had been spooked and wanted to head back. Kaitlyn started laughing.

"Kaitlyn, it's not funny! Move and I'll paddle." Jared tried to convince her.

But seeing Jared in a frenzied state made Kaitlyn laugh harder. The loud uncontrollable laughs rolled across the lake and filled the air. She just kept laughing, barely able to get any words out.

"Jared, I can't." She said between laughs.

He calmed down a little, enough to exclaim, "What!"

Still laughing, Kaitlyn said, "Jared, I just peed my pants."

# EMILY

CRUMBS by Rose White

Emily sat in the crowded stands, holding a seat for a friend. It was a rivalry soccer game between Hope College and Calvin College. People milled around, filling the stadium. There was a clash between those wearing the dark maroon of Calvin and the dark blue and orange of Hope.

But Emily wore an unassuming Michigan sweatshirt—blue and maize. She looked around, searching for her friend while she kept her hand on the seat next to her. Emily turned her head to look behind her and scanned the crowd. Her eyes landed on a man a couple of rows back. Was that Jason Hanson? Former kicker for the Lions and Emily's favorite player.

Emily scrutinized his face for a couple of minutes, trying to decide if it was him or not. Why would he be at Hope soccer game? She kept searching the crowd only to return to the potential Jason, could it be him?

Finally, Emily's friend returned. She had to get some kind of confirmation. "Lauren, is that Jason Hanson?"

Lauren, a non-football fan, replied quickly, "Oh yeah, kicker for the Lions? His son is a freshman on the Hope team." Emily couldn't believe it. Her favorite player was only a couple of rows back.

After a couple of minutes, Emily calmed down enough to stand up and walk over to where Jason was sitting with his wife. She cautiously leaned down and said, "Jason?" He looked up, smiled, and said "Hi."

Emily chatted with him and his wife for a bit, all the while unable to believe this was actually happening. She was making small talk with Jason Hanson. Not wanting to be a distraction, Emily grabbed a quick picture with him and went back to her seat. She continued to watch the game with a smile on her face.

# MY BAD

Stories about embarassing moments

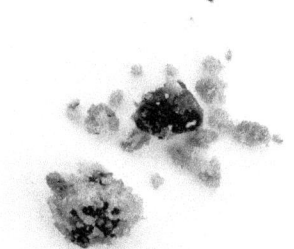

PAM

The room was hot. The steam had nowhere to go, so it settled thickly in the air. Pam leaned against a wall with 50 of her swim teammates as her coach paced around the room. They were squatting, with their knees bent at perfect 90-degree angles. Pam placed her sweaty, burning hands against the cool wall behind her.

She leaned her head against the cement bricks, hoping that small relief would ease her struggle. Pam's face was red from the heat. Her thighs burned and her calves trembled, threatening to give out at any moment. Pam zeroed in on a spot on the ground, focusing on just that small speck of white on the dark ground. This wall sit took all of her strength.

Suddenly, Pam felt her stomach lurch. It swirled and churned inside of her. This was a battle more important than her wall sit. As the seconds ticked by, and her coach walked down her side of the room, he pulled his whistle up to his lips.

He blew the shrill noise, yelling "up!" Pam felt the relief instantly. Her legs relaxed as she straightened them. Her whole body loosened in relief. Her coach was walking by, whistle still in lips when Pam slowly stood up, releasing a loud, unmistakable fart.

# LEVI

**CRUMBS** by Rose White

Eyes squinted and walking slowly, Levi walked out of the oral surgeon's office in a haze. He had just gotten his wisdom teeth out and the medicine hadn't quite worn off yet. His wife, Amber, led him to the car, and they started the drive home.

Levi leaned his head back in the car and mumbled a little to himself. As they continued to drive, he started talking.

"My wife had a bunch of friends over, and the dog threw up her thong."

Amber kept her hands on the wheel, but turned to look at Levi. "What?" she asked.

"My wife had a bunch of friends over, and the dog threw up her thong."

Amber turned away, a little concerned. So, she replied, "Levi, you probably shouldn't be talking. Try biting down on the gauze."

He stopped talking and leaned his head against the window until they got home.

The next several hours were a blur in Levi's memory, but when he reentered the living world, he remembered something strange.

Struggling through the pain, Levi told Amber what the doctor told him right before he went under. Instead of counting down from 10, the surgeon quickly told Levi about when his wife invited a bunch of friends over, and their dog threw up a thong it had eaten.

Levi lay back down, struggling to remember the whole event. And Amber laughed in relief, remembering the weird story Levi repeated in the car.

# RACHEL

Rachel was a prankster. But as March 31 faded into April 1, she started to get nervous. All day she was skittish, expectant, and she tread carefully. But no one pulled a prank on her—not one. As the day wore on, Rachel began to get comfortable and April Fools' slipped from her mind.

She was preparing to leave a church meeting that night and walked out into the parking lot behind the building. Her bright, white car was not where she left it. Rachel was confused; how did someone get her keys? She turned her head left and right scanning the parking lot. Without spotting her car, she tromped around the front of the building, and a group of pranksters followed her. She soon found her car casually parked on the side of the road.

She looked at the group as she unlocked her door, and the group was all still watching her. "Hilarious, guys," she said. Rachel slid into the driver's seat, as her friend Camille hopped into the passenger's seat. Easing her car onto the road, Rachel saw the glow of a phone out of the corner of her eye.

"You're going to film me! Why do you have your phone out!" She yelled in fearful anticipation.

"You're being dramatic." Camille answered still holding her phone.

Not believing her, Rachel pulled to the side of the road got out of the car and said, "Why are you filming me!"

Camille replied, "I'm not!"

Rachel got back into her car and continued to drive. As she merged lanes, she glanced into her rearview mirror. At that moment, she saw a large shadowy figure slowly rise from her trunk, sit up, and silently look at her. Rachel screamed.

It turned out that while someone stole Rachel's keys and moved her car, one of the pranksters hid in her trunk waiting for his chance to scare her. He succeeded.

After that day, Rachel's prankster reputation faded into history.

# KAREN

Karen walked up to the doors of the large grocery store, and they slid open at her presence. A gust of cold air rushed to meet her as she walked into the lobby. A friendly man greeted her, and she smiled back.

Karen looked around the massive building, searching for the pharmacy. She saw it in the distance and hurried over. She dodged in and out of people before finally making it to her destination. It was going to be several minutes before her prescription was ready.

Sitting down on a bench, Karen looked around the busy pharmacy. A group of people—like her—were waiting for prescriptions, but others were just shopping in the nearby aisles. After a couple of minutes, Karen spotted a new blood pressure machine.

She walked over, put her arm in the big sleeve, and looked at the clean, bright screen for instructions. Then a voice spoke out from the computer, "Are you a guy or a gal?" It displayed on the screen the two words, "Guy" and "Gal." Since the machine talked first, Karen responded, "A gal."

"Are you a guy or a gal?"

Karen thought maybe it didn't hear her, so she replied again louder, "A gal."

"Are you are guy or a gal?"

Even louder, Karen said, "A gal!"

At this point, shoppers in the area turned to see what Karen was talking about.

"Are you a guy or a gal?" It asked again.

Keeping her mouth shut this time, Karen reached out and touched the word on the screen. It went onto the next step.

# CHRISTY

Christy and Emma raced down the highway, already late for class. Christy squirmed in her seat; she hated being late. They finally got to the exit, pulled quickly around the corner, and sped into the parking lot where their class was waiting.

Christy whipped open the car door and hurried across the long parking lot. Her new red Converse slapped the pavement as she started speed walking, then jogging, then running.

Meanwhile, Emma had just gotten out of the car and was walking toward the group. She called ahead to Christy, "Why are you running?"

Christy's Converse flashed as she continued to run. "Because we're late!" she yelled back. Then, the front of her new shoe latched onto a little section of raised pavement. Christy fell through the air and landed on her back in a pile of roots.

She lifted her head up, and there was dirt everywhere. Dirt was on her knees, dirt was on her hands, dirt was under her fingernails, dirt was on her chin, and dirt was on the bright, white toes of her shoes.

Christy got to her feet, brushing the dirt off her hands. She looked up and the whole class was laughing at her. And she still had to finish her walk of shame to meet up with them.

# ANA

Ana drove down the sunny Hawaii road with her sunglasses on and the wind rustling her hair. Even though it wasn't legal to use a phone while driving, she casually chatted to a friend on the phone. After a couple of minutes, she saw an island cop behind her on his moped.

He pulled her over to the side of the road and gave her a ticket for using her phone. For this ticket, she had to pay a fee and attend a court date.

The day of her court appearance, Ana was laid out on the couch. Immobility had struck down in the form of mono, and Ana missed the appointment.

A couple of days later, Ana made her way to the courthouse. When she arrived and showed the court clerk her ticket, the person looked it up and said to Ana, "There is a bench warrant out for your arrest."

Shocked, Ana was told she needed to head over to the jail. When she got there, they had to arrest her and put her in jail because she missed her court date. As a formality, they took her mug shot, fingerprinted her, and put her in a cell.

After a couple of minutes, Ana heard the scraping of her cell door open. She followed the guard out and plopped her $100 bail on the counter. Ana had bailed herself out from the small cell in a small jail on a small island in Hawaii.

# LAUREN

CRUMBS by Rose White

Lauren swished her brush in the full container of powdered foundation at the makeup counter. A cloud of shiny beige puffed into the air, and she lifted the brush up to the girl's face. The customer's friend stood nearby watching the process.

Lauren lightly brushed the clean powder on the girl's face with the soft bristles. She carried the brush up the girl's cheeks and lightly covered the skin. Lauren pushed her glasses up on her own clean, clear face and put the brush back in her apron.

Feeling a little uncomfortable, Lauren grabbed a Kleenex to blow her nose. Quietly she blew, but the dribble of snot did not land in her Kleenex. Instead it fell onto her black dress and started to slide down, leaving a light white trail on her dark black dress.

The friend standing nearby said, "That just happened, " and she pointed at Lauren's dress. Lauren looked down and the snot dribble slipped down onto her leg and some fell on the ground. Lauren started laughing and wiped it off her leg.

She looked at the ground and saw a small, shiny puddle of snot on the ground. Still laughing, she dabbed at it with her shoe making a large streak on the floor—only making it worse.

Meanwhile the Kleenex hung unused in her hand.

# KAYLA

**CRUMBS** by Rose White

Twelve-year-old Kayla arrived at the Christian conference grounds for the weeklong summer camp. She walked in with her older brother and sister, and they all sat on the ground with the rest of the 6th-8th graders. The group of about 30 kids formed a circle on the ground and they were instructed to say their names.

Kayla pulled a piece of grass out of the ground and ran it between her fingertips as she waited for her turn to come. She looked up at each kid as they said their names—some loud and clear and some timid. She let the small blade of grass slip out of fingers and fall into the thick grass below.

After the circle was three quarters done, a boy confidently said his name, "Nate." Kayla looked at that boy, maybe he was in seventh grade—or even eighth. But she thought, He's kind of cute. As the circle continued, Kayla kept repeating his name in her brain. Nate. Nate. Nate. Nate. She didn't want to forget, so she could talk to him later.

Nate. Nate. Nate.

The circle was almost at Kayla, and her sister who sat next to her said, "Kendra." There was a small pause, so Kendra nudged Kayla. She came out of her brief memorization bout to say, "Hi. My name is Nate."

There was no recovery. Quickly, she said, "Sorry. My name is Kayla," and the circle continued. Then the circle had to go around again, this time Kayla kept repeating in her mind, My name is Kayla, My name is Kayla, My name is Kayla.

# JONNY

Jonny ran his hands through his hair as he talked to his Grandmother on Skype. His hair was longer than he usually liked it to be.

His friend Keane pulled out clippers. He unwrapped the thick black cord, plugged it into the wall, and put the right length on it. He turned it on, and the blades made a dull whirring noise.

Meanwhile, Jonny sat in the chair talking to his Grandmother on the computer. He updated her on life, talked about the weather, and told her that he needed a haircut. He turned his head at the sound of the clippers, agreeing to let Keane cut his hair.

While Jonny continued chatting with his Grandmother, Keane ran the electric clippers through Jonny's thick, overgrown hair. After a couple of cuts, Keane got down to business. He pushed them into the hair and went straight down the middle of Jonny's head.

Keane looked at the spot in surprise. He had left barely any hair in that section on Jonny's head. Jonny reached his hand up, while still facing the Skype window, and still felt a thin layer of hair. "That's not too bad," he said. So Keane cut the rest of his hair to match.

After Jonny was finished getting the haircut and ended the chat with his Grandmother, he went to the mirror. What he saw staring back was a pale, nearly bald head—barely covered with a thin layer of dark fuzz. Jonny's shoulders drooped and he let out a big sigh. Oh well.

# AMBER

**CRUMBS** by Rose White

Amber and Kain had been dating for awhile, at least, a long time for sixth graders. Everyday Amber's friends asked her, "Have you kissed him yet? Have you kissed? You should kiss him." But everyday, Amber shook her head: no they had not kissed yet.

Finally one day, Amber's friends were fed up. Amber and Kain needed to kiss. So when classes broke and a hoard of students crowded the hallways, Amber met up with Kain. Suddenly, their friends started to circle around them. Amber's friends yelled, "You should kiss him!" and Kain's friends yelled, "You should kiss her!"

Amber felt the circle squeezing in around her as the mob pushed them together. She looked up at the face of her boyfriend, the glint of his braces shining through his small smile. And as the crowd pushed, Amber leaned in. The crowd kept shouting, "Do it! Do it!"

Then, the voices faded away, but the crowd continued to press in. Amber and Kain quickly kissed. In that brief encounter, a bit of Amber's lip got stuck on Kain's braces. So when they pulled away, she felt a sharp pain. Reacting instantly, Amber yelled "Ow! My tooth!" The whole crowd laughed immediately and repeated her line.

The shrill blast of the bell rang, and the group scattered, leaving Amber holding her lip. Alone, she picked up her backpack, slung it over one shoulder, and walked to class.

# ANGELA

Patiently, Angela coached 4-year old Keane through the bible verse that he would recite for the whole church. Each kid was supposed to pick out one verse, memorize it, and share it for the church. Angela helped her son pick out a verse, one that'd would be easy enough for little Keane to remember. They chose John 11:35: Jesus wept.

The week before, Angela would tell Keane the verse and wait for him to repeat it.
She would say, "Keane, remember the verse. 'Jesus wept.'" And Keane would reply in a small voice, "Jesus wept."

One night when they were practicing this, Keane threatened to yell Mr. Poophead in the microphone. Angela chuckled and said to Keane again, "Jesus wept."

After days of practicing, Keane definitely had it down. It was Sunday, and Angela was excited to see her son share his verse in front of everyone. The morning went on, and all the kids were brought up front. Angela straightened up in her chair and looked at the row of kids—Keane was in the middle of the line.

They started at one end, and let each kid speak their verse in the microphone. Proud parents were sprinkled throughout the room, smiling more when their kid spoke out. Angela waited for the microphone to get to Keane.

Suddenly, she remembered the threat. In a last minute panic, she started to warn her friends seated around her. "Keane told me he was going to say Mr. Poophead in the mic!" As the line continued, it felt like time accelerated and slowed down all at once. There was nothing Angela could do but wait.

When it got to Keane, Angela held her breath and her face froze in a half smile. He methodically said, "Jesus wept," and Angela breathed out slightly. Then, he leaned forward, grabbed the microphone, and loudly stated, "Mr. Poophead!"

Angela's smile went from proud parent to uncomfortably frozen. She slid down slightly in her chair and waited for the next verse to start. Angela was shocked, but then again, she wasn't. He had warned her after all.

# LIVING THINGS

Stories about pets and animals

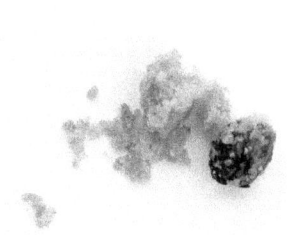

# JESS

## CRUMBS by Rose White

For Jess, it had been a long winter. She spent the cold, grey months cooped up inside her house and inhibited by a large, white, plaster cast around her left leg. After never ending weeks of this, spring made its first appearance.

The sun was shining warmly for the first time in what seemed like years, so Jess, her sister, and her mom headed to the zoo. As soon as she disembarked from the car, Jess hobbled through the gate on her crutches, past the birds, and by the aquarium to get to her favorite animal: the mountain lion.

Jess hopped on one foot, while the other rested slightly above the ground. Her crutches made clicking noises, pushing off the ground and launching Jess forward. The zoo was empty, so the noises of the crutches and Jess' hopping echoed across the wide sidewalks. She tilted her face toward the sun, absorbing the forgotten warmth.

Finally, she reached the mountain lions. Jess approached the wire fence, as one mountain lion paced back and forth right in front of her. She looked to her left, and saw no one; she looked to her right, and saw no one. So she got a little closer, rested her crutch against the fence, and started to reach her hand toward the lion's thick yellow fur.

As she extended her hand, the mountain lion extended his paw, putting it right on the fence. Jess looked at it—the light pink pads under his toes had a layer of dirt on them. All of the sudden, the cat reached its paw through the fence and dug his claws into the rubber topping Jess' crutch.

While standing on her one functional leg, she grabbed the crutch and tried wrestling it away from the mountain lion. She pulled it back, and he pulled it toward him. They kept jerking the crutch back and forth, until Jess' mom came around the corner and started laughing at the sight of Jess playing tug of war with a mountain lion.

Her mom gently eased the crutch away from the cat. Then, it casually sauntered off into the depths of its cage while Jess begrudgingly hopped away on her claw-marked crutches.

# ZOOEY

Zooey quivered a little and ran across the street. She darted in between cars that honked, slammed on their brakes, and swerved out of the way. She tucked her thin black tail between her legs and kept trotting down the road.

At last, Zooey's light brown feet trod on soft grass instead of the rocky, dangerous pavement. She sat down on the ground, opened her mouth, and started breathing heavily. The grass felt cool against her small body, which was still shaking.

Zooey sat there for a couple of minutes letting the cool breeze brush her short fur. Then, a man ran over to her and tried coaxing Zooey over. She started trembling again and ran away. She sprinted across the lawn, avoiding the road.

The man ran after her and followed her across a couple of yards. Zooey pinned her ears back to her head and kept running. Suddenly she found herself cornered with a fence on one side and the man on the other.

She cowered in the corner, trying to hide, but the man scooped her up. He held her tightly and pet her head gently. She was put in the back of a car, driven down the road, and picked up again. She whimpered slightly.

The man opened a door to a house she hadn't been to before. He walked in and placed her on the ground. She stood there for a couple of minutes while the man got Zooey some water. She lapped up a little then walked around.

She laid down in a corner of the house, closed her eyes, stopped shivering, and fell asleep.

# JARED

## CRUMBS by Rose White

The sun had just started to rise, bathing the cold morning in a warm light. Jared leaned back on his car as it filled with gas. The pump lurched slightly when the tank was filled. Jared got back in the car and slipped his sunglasses on.

He turned the key in his ignition and started to drive away. Before Jared could turn onto the main road, he waited for a truck that was driving past. It slowly drove down the road, its wheels making large relaxed rotations.

Jared looked at the truck, and then looked in the other direction. Up ahead, he saw a goose starting to cross the road. It waddled across the path, taking a few small steps. The truck continued to drive down the road, leisurely cruising.

The driver had his mirror down and his sunglasses on, but the sun still shone in his eyes. The goose kept waddling across the road. Then, Jared watched, as the truck did not slow down, but still moved forward. Looking back and forth between the truck and the goose, Jared braced himself as the distance got shorter and shorter. Then the truck ran over the goose.

Shocked, Jared couldn't look away. The goose had disappeared, but when the truck continued to drive at the same speed, Jared just saw a pool of blood on the ground. Disturbed, he finally turned out of the gas station and finished his drive unable to get that image out of his head.

# THE SQUIRREL

**CRUMBS** by Rose White

The squirrel darted around the long stretch of grass that lined the National Mall. He was on a mission. The cool air tousled his fur while he ran. Finally, he spotted what he was looking for: food.

This squirrel had been on the streets of Washington DC for his whole life, and he was a master of mooching off busy tourists. But, he was just coming out of a longer winter, where the tourism was sparse and leftovers were rare.

He began to casually jog over to the girl standing by the food cart. Keeping his speed, her figure slowly got bigger while his stomach seemed to get emptier. The grass squished underneath his feet, so the squirrel picked up his pace.

At last, the squirrel reached the girl. He saw her hand slip into a small, crinkled yellow bag, come out with a bit of food, and place that into her mouth. He started walking up to her, and stopped about a foot away.

He looked up, expecting her to give him a chip. She did not. So he inched a little closer, to the point where he could reach out and touch her scuffed brown shoe. And he did. He put his small hands on the girl's shoes, tipped his head back, and looked at her. She looked at him. Her hand was frozen, stuck inside the chip bag.

He could almost taste the salty, crunchy snack, so he didn't stop. He leaned back on his hind legs and launched into the air. Landing slightly above the girl's knee, he gripped the leg. She screamed and kicked her foot wildly. His little fingers couldn't hold on, and he fell to the ground. He was not going to give up.

He started to charge again, but the girl kept kicking. He dodged in and out of the kicks, until another girl came over and started yelling at him. He backed away, still hungry. The first girl crumpled the bag and threw it in the trash. He leaned back on his hunches and watched them walk away before he turned his head looking out for the next person holding a snack.

# ALLISON

As a freshman in college, Allison and her roommate harbored a pet snake in their dorm room. It was a small 2-foot ball python named Louie. He was mostly black with large brown, Rorschach-like splotches covering his skin.

Louie was spoiled. He often received warm baths, and he had a special chamber where he ate his meals. Also he would only eat live mice—not frozen. One day, Allison's roommate asked her to pick up a mouse on her way home. Louie was hungry.

Allison stopped by a nearby pet store and was greeted by a friendly employee.

He asked, "Is there anything I can help you with?"

Allison replied, "I need to pick up a mouse."

His customer service smile grew larger, and his eyes crinkled in happiness. This employee loved mice. As they made their way to the back of the store, he told Allison about his pet mouse.

He explained that his mouse had gotten quite large, so he was making it a leash to go outside with it. With every word of his story, Allison grew more and more uncomfortable. He was so excited that Allison was also getting a pet mouse.

He reached into the cage and asked Allison, "Boy or girl?" Allison mumbled nothing. Then he picked up a mouse, gently flipped it over in his hand, and said, "This one's a boy. What are you going to name it?"

He dropped in small creature in Allison's hand, and she looked at it her own face reflected in the deep dark eyes of the mouse. She answered, "Sheldon." As Allison left the store, the employee waved happily as if he was saying 'have a great adventure with your new friend.'

Allison took it home, opened the lid to Louie's cage, and dropped the mouse in. She looked away, unable to watch Louie eat Sheldon.

# HANNA

The hair on Persian cats often grows long. Because of this, it needs to be brushed regularly in order to avoid knots and matting. Unfortunately for Hanna's cat, Fiddy, her hair was not brushed. Over time, Hanna noticed the thick clumps of hair and the unkempt mane covering Fiddy's body, so she decided to do something about.

After having perused Pinterest, Hanna wanted to cut Fiddy's hair so that she would just have fur on her face and poms on her feet and tail. But because her hair was so long, Hanna started out with scissors. She grabbed a chunk of fur on Fiddy's back and the satisfying sound of the two blades swiping against each other left a small clump of hair in Hanna's hand. She tried to continue cutting the fur, but Fiddy did not like the scissors.

After taking a few chunks of hair off the cat's back, Fiddy still was not pleased. Her mouth turned down in a permanent frown and she squealed continuously. At this point, Hanna looked into minor sedation for cats. A few sites she looked into recommended a small dose of Benadryl for calming cats down. Hanna filled a small plastic syringe with the suggested cat dosage, squirted it into Fiddy's throat, and foam began to pour out her mouth.

Panicking, Hanna tried to figure out what to do, unaware that when cats eat something that they don't like, they foam at the mouth. But the Benadryl did not help Hanna. She also tried to use the clippers in an attempt to smooth out the mess that was Fiddy's back. Hanna managed to buzz off the hair on her tail, leaving a puff of fur at the end, but the cat was not willing to allow anymore of this haircutting. Fiddy squealed. Fiddy struggled. Fiddy did not like the clippers.

Hanna had to give up. Fiddy was left with mangled, chopped up fur on her back, her tail was thin with a puff at the end, and her front was still full of fur. At this point, all Hanna hoped for was for Fiddy to become a famous Pinterest fail.

# COLTON

Colton sat in the black plastic chair that was perched atop the riding lawn mower. It smelled of old cut grass and gasoline. Small bits of grass shavings were dried onto the side of the green mower and its black debris shield.

Colton turned the key, and the trusty mower started right up. The smell of gasoline flooded the air. Colton steered the mower over to the corner of the yard and started making laps around the grass. The job was methodical.

He relaxed a bit in the chair, letting his back slump against the seat as he steered the mower gently with two hands. He carefully followed his tracks in the grass, keeping the lines straight and crisp.

All of the sudden, a chipmunk ran down a tree and into the yard. In its fear of the mower, it ran right in front of Colton before he had a chance to shut off the machine. It got caught in the blades, and Colton quickly turned the key, shutting the mower off. But he wasn't fast enough. Instead, he heard the chipmunk get caught in the blades and come out the other side.

Colton winced. But, there was nothing he could do. He turned the key again, letting the machine roar to life. He continued in his cutting, once again following the tracks. He completed a couple more laps, when a snake slithered out in front of the mower. Without time to react, it also got sucked up into the blades. This time, Colton didn't look back and didn't turn the machine off. Instead, he hoped for the best.

After he completed the next lap, he drove past what remained the snake. It didn't even have a chance.

# MARILYN

CRUMBS by Rose White

Marilyn was taking her small tan and white dog named Draper for a walk in her small village. It was late winter, so there were still mounds dirt covered snow. But the air held the warm promise of spring as the sun stayed out later and later. It was a brisk walk in the cool dusk, and the two started on the way back home.

They were nearing the end of their walk when Marilyn heard a woman yelling, "Pick up your dog! Pick up your dog! My dog will attack!" Marilyn looked into the distance to see a large dusky Great Dane barreling toward them.

Marilyn's small pup was too far away to just pick him up, so she pulled the leash in close enough to just pick him up off the ground. Draper dangled from the air just as the Great Dane came up to them and started growling. From the ai,r, Draper barked loudly at the Great Dane struggling to attack.

In order to keep Draper away from the giant dog, Marilyn swung Draper around her in the air. Meanwhile, he kept growling and barking trying to threaten the much larger dog. Finally, the Dane was called back. Marilyn put a rattled Draper on the ground and the two calmly walked back home.

Draper flew that day.

# GOING PLACES

Stories about travel

# LAURA

**CRUMBS** by Rose White

Laura and her husband Dan spent a week helping her sister move down to Costa Rica. There was a lot of babysitting, a lot of planning, and a lot of doing. So despite being so close to the equator, Laura and Dan didn't have the chance to do very many tropical activities. Until they went ziplining.

It was the rainy season in Costa Rica, which meant the air was damp and thick. This kept the tourists away. So it was just Dan, Laura, two tour guides, and one dog, named Charlie who all heading into the jungle.

They hiked up a trail, following behind Charlie, whose thick, dark brown fur shined with water. Charlie had been an abandoned puppy who the tour guides had found hungry, lost, and tired in the mountains. But, over the years, he was well fed and spent much up his time running up and down the thickly forested mountains of the Costa Rican jungle. Now, he was a strong and handsome dog.

They finally got to the zipline, and Charlie waited below, looking up with his dark eyes. Laura set off on the zipline and the chocolate lab bounded beneath her. The wind pushed the hair off Laura's face, and she looked down to see dense arrays of water, pulling together into clouds. Some of the trees poked through these white blocks, but for the most part it was a cloud forest.

Occasionally, though, there would be a break between the fog and the trees, and Laura would glance down to see Charlie darting across the mountain still leading the way.

# ELIJAH

**CRUMBS** by Rose White

While backpacking through Europe, Elijah made a three-day stop in Rome. On the last day, he did what he had wanted to do for a long time: see the Colosseum. When he got there, Elijah barely snagged a last minute ticket to get inside and followed the tour group in.

When they walked in, Elijah looked around at the massive crumbling structure, imagining the history that had taken place here. He wandered around taking pictures of the wonder.

Elijah had ambled over to the pedestal where the winners would stand. There was a circular, elevated piece of sculpted stone that sat atop a section of bricks. Elijah looked at them and noticed that some of the bricks were loose.

Taking out his camera, Elijah pointed it upward and took a few photos. Then he kneeled down and pretended to take some photos of the bricks. Instead, Elijah picked up a six-inch by six-inch crumbled brick and slipped it into his satchel.

Standing back up, he flipped the top of his satchel on his bag and patted the brick. He finished strolling around the Colosseum and left without any questions. But he did walk out with a 2,000-year old piece of history.

The whole flight home, Elijah kept the brick in his bag under the seat in front of him. When he got back to the States, he felt his heart beat a little faster and his palms got a little sweaty when he went through customs. But he passed through without any problems.

It's been ten years, and that brick has gone with Elijah everywhere. Currently, a piece of the Colosseum sits on his coffee table in Michigan, thousands of miles away from its origin.

**SYDNEY**

Sydney was an American in Ireland.

She was spending the summer nannying for a young family, who conveniently lived within a two-mile walking distance of the Ireland rail service called DART.

On a cloudy Sunday morning, she set out to adventure. Flipping through travel guides, she recognized the name of a small town called Howth. Seemingly unremarkable, she only went that way because her host family had recommended it a few weeks earlier.

The train eased out of the bustling Dublin city center and headed toward the coast. For nearly an hour, it rumbled across the rail tracing the blue ocean and the green country. Eventually the brakes squealed and the cars began to slow. It was the final stop, and an automated voice warned, "Mind the gap between the train and the platform edge."

Sydney navigated her way out of the small station just as a light rain started. She looked out at the small village of Howth but quickly passed through the center of the town and just kept walking. After a brisk stroll, she ran into a path that was supposed to lead the ocean, and she followed it over to some looming hills.

Sydney stretched out her legs, increasing her a gait. Her black leather boots glided over the wet grass as they picked up bits of water along the way. The sun had emerged and the temperature warmed, so she pulled down the hood of her bright rain coat. Sydney's path continued, and after about a mile, she literally reached the edge of a cliff.

She peered to her left and saw a stretch of rock faces and steep drop-offs, and in the distance sat a small lighthouse. For a quiet Sunday afternoon in Ireland, this was exactly what Sydney had wanted to see. She smiled and kept walking.

# JESS

# CRUMBS by Rose White

Sushi is like popcorn. People will settle for microwave popcorn, eat it, and enjoy it. But, when they eat movie theatre popcorn, it's not even comparable. Likewise, people will settle for average sushi, but when they get to eat authentic Japanese cuisine, it's like eating sushi for the first time.

Sushi was one of the reasons Jess was so excited to go to Japan. Yes, there were other motivating factors, but the sushi was what she was looking forward to the most.

After being in Japan for some time, Jess and her two friends stumbled upon a sushi restaurant that would give them the authentic experience and food that she had been looking forward too. The expectancy that had built up over the past few months had reached its summit.

Jess ordered her sushi and waited for the small rolls of pure white rice surrounded by the nearly black outer shell to be placed in front of her. When the long white plate came, she picked up her chopsticks and placed a roll on her tongue. Jess bit down, releasing the heat of wasabi into her watering mouth.

Not wanting to spit out the roll, she chewed as fast as she could, swallowed, and gulped down some water. The burn from the wasabi emanated from her mouth through her nose, and it felt like it went from the front of her forehead all the way to the top of her head. Jess thought her brain was on fire.

It took hours for the heat to disseminate, but at least Jess got to have authentic Japanese sushi.

# MONICA

While a missionary in Cameroon in Central Africa, Monica was sent out to invite the locals to a drama evangelism event. Monica strolled through the streets under the hot sun with flyers in her hand, a friend, and a large Cameroonian man by her side. Monica's friend was tall and had fiery red hair—she stood out in the crowd.

They stopped a couple of times to talk to some people and hand them an invite. Monica and the other girl walked up to a man standing on the side of the dusty road, but instead of grabbing the piece of paper, the man grabbed Monica's wrist.

He held her arm tightly; his fingers were wrapped around Monica's small wrist. He started yelling "What! What! What are you going to do? What are you going to do?" With each yell, the piece of paper in Monica's hand rustled a little.

Unsure of how to respond, Monica just started waving the small invite in front of his face by whipping her wrist back and forth. The man kept his grip. Monica could feel her tall friend shuffle behind her, crouching down.

Then after what felt like an eternity, the Cameroonian man who had been with the girls walked up to the stranger who was gripping Monica's arm. He said a simple, "Bonjour," and crossed his arms. The man released his hand, and Monica regained her composure, handed him an invite, and stretched her wrist out.

# BRYCE

At the beginning of the winter break from college, Bryce and his girlfriend set out to explore Chicago. It was their first time heading to the city, so they wanted to ensure they would have enough time to explore.

At 4:00am on December 17, they slid into a cold car and began their journey. They drove through the darkness for a couple of hours and boarded a 6:00am train to Chicago. It rumbled through the south side of the city, and time went back an hour.

Unaware of the time change, which placed them right in the middle of rush hour, the two awkwardly stood on the train clutching anything to help maintain their balance. But they kept bumping into business people with their backpacks. Surrounded by men and women clad in black, dark blue, and grey, Bryce and Bryn stood out in their jeans and bright coats.

The train reached the city after barreling through the still, dark morning at 7am. Bryce and Bryn slowly got off the train and let the sea of people rush around them. It wasn't long before they were the only two trying to make their way out of the underground station, just searching for a glimpse of light.

Finally, they found the stairs that led them into the dim city, most of which was still asleep. It was a brisk seven degrees outside, but it was also too early for anything to be open yet. So Bryce and Bryn strolled over to Millennium Park to see the bean. They stood there, stomping their feet, letting out small puffs of hot air into the frozen morning. It was mostly quiet, other than the dull roar of traffic and the rustling noises coming from a photographer nearby.

After a few minutes, the sun began to rise. The bean reflected the weak rays. The shiny surface would, later in the day, mirror hundreds of tourists distorted faces. But for now, it simply cast the morning sun back into the sky. Bryce and Bryn then made their way across the empty beach and wandered over to The Shedd Aquarium.

The Shedd opened at 9, yet even after meandering throughout the city, the two were still 15 minutes early. They pulled their coats tighter and stood by a Korean couple who was also early. Both sets of people made slight eye contact and smiled tentatively. They just waited and smiled.

When it finally opened, Bryce, Bryn, and the Korean couple were the only people in the aquarium for the first hour. They didn't run into each other again.

The Shedd has over 2 million visitors each year, but for the small price of nearly freezing, Bryce and Bryn got to experience it practically alone.

**EMMA**

Emma's aunt handed her and her sister, Sarah, a steaming cup of fresh coffee. Thick, lush trees and small campsites surrounded them in an upstate New York campground. Emma's aunt put her hand over her eyes, peering around and said, "Well, I'm going to go look for everyone else. Will you stay here, and I'll call you when I've found them?"

"Sure," Emma replied, shrugging her shoulders and taking a sip of coffee.

Emma and Sarah put their feet up by the fire chatting easily. After about 30 minutes, the coffee dwindled, and Emma looked at her phone. There was no cell service. She scrunched her eyebrows together and looked up at Sarah.

"How can Aunt Joan call us if we have no service? Who wants to be here if she found everyone and forgot about us."

Sarah nodded in agreement, so the two set off to go find the rest of their family. They wandered around the campsite and the adjoining woods for a couple of hours, searching for anything familiar. After only spotting tall trees and mulched forest ground, Emma figured they should look in other the campground.

Emma and Sarah trekked up to the main road and walked alongside the cracked white shoulder line. They hadn't quite made it to the other campground, when a car pulled up next to them. Emma's dad rolled down the window and said, "There you are! We've been looking for you!"

He drove them to the main campground, and their aunt came up to the car. "I forgot that I left you there!" Emma shrugged, at least there had been coffee.

**ELISABETH**

There was a thick humidity in the Philippine air that made even the mosquitos fly slower. One fat mosquito lazily made its way over to Elisabeth's hand as she squirted sunscreen into her skin. She swatted it away and rubbed the white cream between her hands. Then she dabbed the SPF 80 onto her face, her arms, her chest, her legs, her feet, and anything with the potential to be exposed to the sun.

When Elisabeth was done, she stepped out into the hot Philippine sun. Her tennis shoes squelched in the mud that never seemed to dry. Pulling her feet out of the muck, she walked toward the small orphanage up the road.

Elisabeth creaked open the door to the building, stepped in, and squinted to see in the dim lighting. She took a couple more steps in, and some small girls ran up to her. They ran their small, brown fingers over Elisabeth's clear, porcelain skin, barely skimming their fingertips on her arms.

Then the girls looked up at Elisabeth with their brown eyes open wide in amazement. "Beautiful skin," one would say. "Beautiful skin," another would echo. They crowded in wonderment around Elisabeth to see the pale skin that—much to Elisabeth's chagrin—would stubbornly refuse to tan during the summer.

# JUSTIN

**CRUMBS** by Rose White

In the middle of a yearlong world traveling trip, Justin and Shawnna had arrived in Portugal. They picked up their rental car, a small white, VW polo for less than 60 euros. Once they hoisted their luggage into the car, Justin drove to the farm they would be staying on.

Justin mapped out the destination with Google Maps, which took him on a winding route through the small village of Aljezur. The car weaved down the road, with porches on one side and a guardrail on the other. A few minutes into the journey, Justin noticed that the road kept getting narrower and narrower.

The porches grow closer to the guardrail and the paved path shrunk the farther they drove. Justin thought, this might not be meant for cars, but there was a guardrail—so he kept on driving. The street kept winding with sharp turns and small buffers.

After squeezing down the road, a man ran out of his house and onto the porch facing the road. He yelled, "No! No! Not a road!" Justin stopped the car, but there was nowhere to turn around and backing out would be filled with sharp turns.

The man offered to help Justin back all the way back down the non-road. Carefully, the two communicated through hand signals and yelling. Justin eased the car backward, turning the car left and right around bends in the road. He barely had six inches on the side of the car for mistakes.

Finally, there was one more turn before getting back onto a real road. The car didn't turn quite right, the bumper hit the guardrail, and the car got scratched. At the end of the week, the scratch cost an extra 190 euros.

What was going to be a really cheap deal on a car, ended up being a lot of money.

# MICHELLE

**CRUMBS** by Rose White

It was a box of leftovers.

A box of forgotten leftovers that was baking in the sun from for eight hours in 75-degree weather.

Michelle and her co-workers had just climbed back into the van, ready to return home from a long conference. They all settled in, and someone put their backpack on the ground. Suddenly, the van was filled with the stench of old, steamy Mexican food.

No one knew where the smell was coming from. Instead, they opted to just open their windows and let the breeze waft the smell away. But it lingered. Until someone found the box.

The driver wanted to pull over, but they were travelling as a convoy and following another car. They couldn't stop and throw it out without getting lost. Instead, at every stop on the way to the highway, the driver tried encouraging people to open the door and leave it on the side of the road.

No one stepped up to the challenge.

Eventually, the van rumbled onto the highway, and the wind from the windows became unbearably strong. The people in the van started yelling at each other.

"Hand me the box!" The driver yelled.

Michelle passed the box to him, and the front seat passenger reached over and took the wheel. The driver opened the box and tipped it out the window.

The 70mph highway gusts picked up the pico, the tomatoes, the lettuce, and the cheese and threw it back into the car. The explosion mainly hit Michelle as food shrapnel peppered all the passengers. Lettuce was everywhere, cheese had made it to the back row, and one tomato slice was plastered to the back window.

Unsuccessful, the driver passed the box back with everything that still remained—the taco shells, the meat, the beans— everything except for the toppings that now littered the van.

# CATHERINE

Catherine tromped over to her tent, letting her flashlight bounce off the hardened dirt path. It was her first Canadian camping trip, and she was ready to have a successful adventure. But, no one told her you shouldn't keep snacks in your tent.

Having reached her tent, Catherine knelt down, gripped the small zipper, and began to open the door. Once it was partly open, she heard a light rustling sound. Fearful, Catherine tried shining her small flashlight in the tent, but she couldn't see anything.

Yelling down to her friends at a bonfire, Catherine exclaimed, "I think there's something in my tent!" It took a couple of minutes, but finally someone came up, peered into the tent, and said, "There's a baby raccoon in there!"

Catherine and her friend poked their heads into the tent and gawked at two little raccoons curled up on Catherine's pillow. They both gazed at the small creatures, acknowledging their cuteness. The raccoons breathed deeply and their chests went up and down in their slumber.

They didn't want to disturb the little creatures, but Catherine needed her tent back. Together, they slowly moved the small masked animals out into the woods before Catherine climbed into her sleeping bag and zipped her tent up before curling up and falling asleep.

**SHAWNNA**

The subway zipped through the underground of Seoul in South Korea. It flew by the lights lining the tunnel so fast that they just seemed like a bright blur. The car was full, but Shawnna had luckily found a seat.

She looked out the window across from her, seeing the grey cement and the blurred lights pass by. The train surged forward, accelerating quickly. As it fell into a steady rhythm, Shawnna looked over at the man next to her.

His eyelids were drooping, and he slouched on the seat—drunk. The train started to slow, approaching the next stop. It lurched, putting the brakes on, and stopped. A crowd got off the train and another crowd got on. The man's head fell a little closer to Shawnna's shoulder.

The train jumped again, zooming towards the next stop. The man's head kept dropping more and more until he rested against Shawnna's shoulder. She nudged him, trying to wake him up, but he slept on. Finally, Shawnna stood up, letting him drop to the seat.

She stood in the middle of the car, holding onto the strap above her head. The car raced through the tunnel, until it came to a quick stop at the next station. When the doors slid open, two men jumped on board, grabbed the drunk man, and dragged him off the train.

Shawnna sat back down.

# HANNAH

While living in Africa, Hannah helped in a small school for preschoolers through kindergarteners. Hannah spent most of her time in the smaller class. Everyday, each little student would bring their own lunch to school, and everyone gathered together in a large room to eat.

Hannah was surprised at how this process differed from lunch in the States. The teachers would go around the room and force the kids to eat their food. This would include the teachers and helpers walking around to each student, sitting next to them, and ensuring the food was eaten.

One day Hannah was helping out at lunch, and she walked over to a small girl eating chicken and cornmeal. Sitting next to her, Hannah encouraged her to keep eating. After a couple of bites, the young girl stopped eating. She looked up at Hannah, her face twisting in uncertainty. Suddenly the girl puked all over Hannah's skirt.

She picked her head up, looked at Hannah again, and started eating again. Hannah started to clean up her skirt and the floor, when another teacher came over and started to ensure the girl finished eating.

Hannah wiped her skirt and walked away as the girl swallowed the last bites of her lunch.

# HEIDI

Heidi and a group of five other international students living in Spain hopped on a large bus to Valencia. It was a brisk, sunny Halloween morning; a holiday Heidi had forgotten about in the course of her travels.

After a long bus ride, Heidi and her friends finally arrived at their destination. They were meeting up with another friend who was already at the hostel in the city. She grabbed her backpack and walked down the stairs into the new city.

Heidi looked up at some of the buildings and breathed in the smell of a place she had never been before. The group started walking down the streets that were laced with a kind of history that the United States doesn't have.

The streets were crowded, and Heidi bumped into a passerby. She turned around to apologize and just saw a grey face covered in rivulets of dried blood. The zombie smiled at her with rotten teeth and walked away.

Frightened, Heidi turned back around and looked at the rest of the people on the street. She saw grey face after grey face, some wearing torn clothes, some limping, and some running.

Heidi and her friends wandered around the city for hours, searching for their hostel. Heidi kept bumping into zombies, turning to apologize, and being frightened by the person she faced. The city of Valencia was brimming with the undead for Halloween.

After three hours of wandering, Heidi and her friends finally found their hostel. They walked in and collapsed on their beds. Exhausted but unable to fall asleep, Heidi's mind was filled with dead, zombie-like faces.

# THE BESTS

## CRUMBS by Rose White

The sun rose on the Best's family road trip to Canada.

7:30 came. Josh, April, Frederick, and Edith were out the door and ready to drive. They just had a few quick stops to make on the way: the grocery store, breakfast at Tim Horton's, and gas.

As the early morning sun started to beam down on their car, Josh dropped April off at the store and drove over to Tim Horton's. Each quickly got what they needed, met back up, and headed over to the gas station.

April hopped out of the car, unscrewed the gas cap, and began to fill the tank of their gleaming black car. After a few minutes, the pump abruptly stopped, and April reached to put the cap back on. At that moment, Josh asked her, "Can you clean the back window?"

With rapid movements, April wiped it down and slid back into the car eager to get the trip started. Leaning back in the seat, she picked up her coffee, blew on it, and took a sip as she pulled the car onto the road. After a minute of driving on the highway, they heard a clunking sound. Both quickly realized it was the gas cap, hanging loosely from a thin string. Before they had a chance to react, the noise stopped, and the cap bounced down the lonely highway.

Josh pulled out his phone and searched to determine if it was unsafe to drive without a gas cap. One forum said, "It is extremely dangerous to drive without a gas cap because a cigarette butt could land in your open tank and blow up the car. It is worth it for the safety of your car."

It seemed worth it to buy a new one, so Josh looked up the cost. "Approximately $100."

Begrudgingly, Josh and April came to the decision that they would just spend the money and try to continue their road trip.

They stopped at an auto store, brought the cap, and put it on the car. As Josh climbed in, April asked how much it cost.

"$10."

Finally, at 8:24, the car pulled back onto the highway and began its journey.

Moral of the story: the Internet exaggerates.

Kristen shifted her weight from foot to foot as she waited for her section to board the plane. Finally, the flight attendant made the call. Excitedly, Kristen walked up, handed over her ticket, and walked the long elevated stretch across the tarmac.

After she got settled, Kristen put her seatbelt on and noticed the small boy sitting next to her. He was probably about seven or eight, and he was sitting by himself. Kristen leaned over and said hi. They talked for a little bit about where he was going (Zimbabwe), where his family was (he was in foster care), and what his name was (Israel).

At this point, the plane was coasting through the air and the seatbelt sign had been turned off. Israel looked at Kristen with his wide brown eyes and asked her, "Can you do the splits?"

Kristen shrugged, "Maybe! I could when I was like five."

Israel looked away and said, "I tried, but I hurt my peanuts."

Kristen laughed, and so did Israel.

Then he asked her another question, "Will you do cartwheels with me?"

Kristen looked up and saw the drink cart coming down the aisle. She said, "Israel look! It's a submarine!"

She ducked down behind the seats and pretended to hide from the metal cart. Israel grinned and ducked behind the seats too. The stewardess quickly pushed the cart to the section behind them and started handing out drinks. As she made her way up the row, Kristen and Israel were spying on the submarine-cart. When it came by them, they were silent—hiding.

Kristen and Israel spent the rest of the flight playing games, running up the aisles, and hiding

## CRUMBS by Rose White

from the large stainless steel carts. At the end of the long journey, the plane landed on the runway. Kristen looked at Israel and said, "Well, this is where I get off."

When they got off the plane, they both started to head to their next destination. After a couple of steps, Kristen heard Israel saying her name. She turned around and he ran up to her, "I hope I see you again," he said.

Kristen smiled, and replied, "I hope I see you again too!"

# ABOUT THE AUTHOR

By day, Rose White is a reporter in West Michigan. By night, she's a writer, book editor and frankly, a bit of a nerd. A Michigan native, she studied writing at Grand Valley State University and earned a master's degree in journalism from the University of the West of England. She is also a lover of all things sweet, so there are always crumbs nearby. This is her first published book.

global giving initiative

In pursuit of our mission to help people get their voices and ideas out into the world, we realize that others are concerned with more pressing needs. Finding creativity in every person is important work, but getting food, shelter, and dignity to individuals must come first. That's why Unprecedented Press donates a portion of all book launch revenue to the Everyone Gobal Giving Initative whose goal is to meet the practical needs of individuals around the world and to share the love of Jesus. To learn more, visit everyoneglobal.com

# Other titles from Unprecedented Press

40 Shocking Facts for 40 Weeks of Pregnancy - Volume 1:
*Disturbing Details about Childbearing & Birth*

By Joshua Best

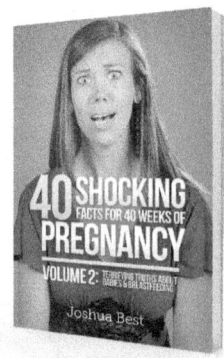

40 Shocking Facts for 40 Weeks of Pregnancy - Volume 2:
*Terrifying Truths about Babies & Breastfeeding*

By Joshua Best

She Can Laugh
*A Guide to Living Spiritually, Emotionally & Physically Healthy*

By Melissa Lea Hughes

Once Upon A Year
*Experience a year in the life of Finn*

By Joanna Lenau

Y - Christian Millennial Manifesto
*Addressing Our Strengths and Weaknesses to Advance the Kingdom of God*

Y, The Workbook
*A Companion*

By Joshua Best

All titles available from Amazon
or from unprecedentedpress.com/shop

www.ingramcontent.com/pod-product-compliance
Lightning Source LLC
Chambersburg PA
CBHW060455300426
44113CB00016B/2596